LOGIC PROGRAMMING:
OPERATIONAL SEMANTICS AND PROOF THEORY

Distinguished Dissertations in Computer Science

Edited by
C.J. van Rijsbergen, University of Glasgow

The Conference of Professors of Computer Science (CPCS) in conjunction with the British Computer Society (BCS), selects annually for publication up to four of the best British Ph.D. dissertations in computer science. The scheme began in 1990. Its aim is to make more visible the significant contribution made by Britain - in particular by students - to computer science, and to provide a model for future students. Dissertations are selected on behalf of CPCS by a panel whose members are:

M. Clint, Queen's University, Belfast
R.J.M. Hughes, University of Glasgow
R. Milner, University of Edinburgh (Chairman)
K. Moody, University of Cambridge
M.S. Paterson, University of Warwick
S. Shrivastava, University of Newcastle upon Tyne
A. Sloman, University of Birmingham
F. Sumner, University of Manchester

LOGIC PROGRAMMING: OPERATIONAL SEMANTICS AND PROOF THEORY

JAMES H. ANDREWS
Simon Fraser University

CAMBRIDGE
UNIVERSITY PRESS

PUBLISHED BY THE PRESS SYNDICATE OF THE UNIVERSITY OF CAMBRIDGE
The Pitt Building, Trumpington Street, Cambridge, United Kingdom

CAMBRIDGE UNIVERSITY PRESS
The Edinburgh Building, Cambridge CB2 2RU, UK
40 West 20th Street, New York NY 10011–4211, USA
477 Williamstown Road, Port Melbourne, VIC 3207, Australia
Ruiz de Alarcón 13, 28014 Madrid, Spain
Dock House, The Waterfront, Cape Town 8001, South Africa

http://www.cambridge.org

First published 1992
First paperback edition 2004

A catalogue record for this book is available from the British Library

ISBN 0 521 43219 7 hardback
ISBN 0 521 60754 X paperback

Contents

Abstract

Logic programming systems which use parallel strategies for computing "and" and "or" are theoretically elegant, but systems which use sequential strategies are far more widely used and do not fit well into the traditional theory of logic programming. This thesis presents operational and proof-theoretic characterisations for systems having each of the possible combinations of parallel or sequential "and" and parallel or sequential "or".

The operational semantics are in the form of an abstract machine. The four control strategies emerge as simple variants of this machine with varying degrees of determinism; some of these variants have equivalent, compositional operational semantics, which are given.

The proof-theoretic characterisations consist of a single central sequent calculus, LKE (similar to Gentzen's sequent calculus for classical first order logic), and sets of axioms which capture the success or failure of queries in the four control strategies in a highly compositional, logical way. These proof-theoretic characterisations can be seen as logical semantics of the logic programming languages.

The proof systems can also be used in practice to prove more general properties of logic programs, although it is shown that they are unavoidably incomplete for this purpose. One aspect of this incompleteness is that it is not possible to derive all valid sequents having free variables; however, induction rules are given which can help to prove many useful sequents of this kind.

Acknowledgements

Thank you:

To the British Science and Engineering Research Council, Edinburgh University, the Edward Boyle Memorial Trust, and Bell-Northern Research Inc., for their generous financial assistance;

To my advisors, Don Sannella and Stuart Anderson, for many fruitful meetings;

To Inge-Maria Bethke, Ruth Davis, Paul Gilmore, Lars Hallnäs, James Harland, Bob Harper, Gordon Plotkin, David Pym, Peter Schroeder-Heister, and David Walker, for helpful comments and suggestions;

To Paul Voda, for his vision and for setting me on the course of research that led to this thesis;

To my examiners, Alan Smaill and Dov Gabbay, for very helpful corrections and suggestions;

And to Julian Bradfield, Leslie Henderson, Jane Hillston, Craig McDevitt, James McKinna, and the Salisbury Centre Men's Group, for much-appreciated friendship and support.

This thesis is dedicated to the memory of my father, Stewart James Andrews.

Chapter 1

Introduction

The quest for programming languages which are more readable and expressive has led to many developments in programming languages, one of which is the logic programming paradigm. In theory, logic programming languages are more readable and expressive because they borrow some of the expressive power of the language of mathematical logic – a language which was developed specifically in order to model some of the deductive processes of the human mind.

This theoretical goal has been achieved to only a limited extent in practice, because the implementations of logic programming languages differ from the ideal theoretical model in many ways. One of the most basic and profound of the differences is that the theory concerns languages which can be implemented completely only by parallel (breadth-first) interpreters, while most practical implementations use incomplete, sequential (depth-first) strategies.

This incompleteness in itself would not necessarily be a problem; but unfortunately, the exact set of terminating sequential logic programs is hard to characterise in a logical way. Sequentiality also affects reasoning about programs, disrupting the hope that the identification of program with logical formula would make this straightforward. These problems tend to weaken claims that practical and truly logical programming is possible.

This thesis is intended as a step towards mending this rift between theory and practice, between parallel and sequential systems. In the thesis, I present a homogeneous operational characterisation of the parallel and sequential versions of a basic logic programming language; I then use proof systems to characterise, in a logical manner, the sets of queries which terminate in the various parallel, sequential, and mixed control disciplines. I also show how these proof systems can be used to prove more general properties of logic programs.

By way of introduction, I will present some discussion about the general principles and historical development of programming languages and semantics. I then will focus on logic programming, addressing in particular the various approaches to its declarative and operational semantics, and the associated problems. Finally, I will delineate the approach and scope of this thesis, and end this introduction with some definitional preliminaries.

1. Programming Languages and Semantics

In the first computer languages, programs consisted of sequences of encoded instructions which described how the computer was supposed to change its internal state at each step of the computation. These languages were very "machine-oriented", in the sense that they expressed directly what the machine was to do. To write a program, programmers had to find out how to express the problem to be solved as a sequence of instructions.

Programmers soon came to realise that certain constructs corresponding to higher-level concepts were being used again and again. Compilers and interpreters were introduced in order to allow programmers to express these higher-level concepts more directly, with the compiler or interpreter handling the automatic translation into the standard constructs: languages thus became more "human-oriented". For instance, in FORTRAN, programmers were for the first time able to write arithmetic expressions directly, and expect the compiler to generate the appropriate sequence of loads, stores and arithmetic operations.

The concepts of procedures and functions, structured programming, functional, logic, and object-oriented programming all arose out of similar desires to make high-level concepts clearer. Languages can now be grouped into various so-called "paradigms", according to how a program is viewed in the language. In imperative languages, a program is a sequence of instructions. In functional languages, it is a set of formal declarations of functions. In logic programming languages, it is a set of logical expressions acting as a "knowledge base". And in object-oriented languages, it is a description of communications between agents.

To some extent, semantics of programming languages reflect the desire to view programs at a high level. One important thing that a formal semantics can give us is an abstract mathematical account of the exact sense in which a programming language encodes higher-level concepts. Thus, functional programming language semantics associate function definitions with actual mathematical functions; logic programming language semantics associate programs with models, which in turn are characterisations of "possible states of knowledge". A good semantics describes rigorously how we expect programs to behave at a high level, and does so in terms of the intended paradigm.

However, in addition to a high-level view, we still need descriptions of programming languages which capture what is going on at the basic level within the machine. We need such descriptions in order to tell how much time and space our programs are going to take up and how we can improve our programs' efficiency, and in order to be able to follow the execution of our programs for debugging and testing purposes.

These computational considerations are somewhat in conflict with the other purposes of semantics. The way in which we usually resolve this conflict is to give one "operational" semantics which meets our computational criteria, and one or more other semantics which give a higher-level, "declarative" view of the meanings of programs. We then formally prove the equivalence of the two semantic descriptions, to allow us to get the benefits of both.

2. Logic Programming

In logic programming, in particular, the tradition since the earliest papers in semantics [74] has been to give an operational (or "procedural") semantics (usually based on SLD-resolution [45]), and one or more logical (or "declarative") semantics which give intuitive descriptions of the meanings of programs. The operational semantics, however, is usually implemented only incompletely, so if we want to keep the correspondence between operational and declarative semantics we must find new declarative semantics which correspond to the incomplete implementations.

2.1. Declarative Semantics

The declarative semantics of logic programming is a reflection of what we want to use logic programming for. Some programming tasks have an inherently logical nature, such as knowledge-based systems and automated theorem provers. Other tasks, such as protocol testers and definite clause grammar parsers, are not immediately logical but are easily expressed in logic. The language of formal logic was developed specifically in order to express such ideas symbolically, particularly in the realm of mathematics; its semantics, model theory, is based on mathematical structures which reflect notions of *a priori* and derived truth. Thus, when we write a logic program, we have (if we understand logic and its model theory) a clear intuitive idea of what it means.

The traditional approach to logic programming semantics [74, 50, 33] views a program as a set of logical formulae (Horn clauses). The "denotation" of the program is the least model of this set of formulae; a query to the program is satisfiable iff some closed instance of it is in the least model. It is the intention that the operational semantics, when given a program and a query, finds a satisfying substitution to the query if one exists. In the traditional approach, there is also a fixpoint semantics which acts as a "bridge" between the operational and declarative semantics, for the purpose of proving soundness and completeness properties of the operational semantics.

There is also a more minor tradition of *proof-theoretic characterisation* of logic programs [41, 42, 5]. One goal of this approach is to combine the logicalness of model-theoretic descriptions with the precision and formality of operational descriptions. A proof-theoretic characterisation associates a program with a proof system with respect to which the operational semantics is sound and complete. The soundness and completeness typically takes the following form: a query is successful iff an associated formula is a theorem of the proof system.

Proof-theoretic characterisations have several advantages. As in least model semantics, programs are described in terms of the logic underlying our intuitions about programs. But unlike model-theoretic approaches, the characterisation is purely formal and syntactic, so the proofs of soundness and completeness can be purely syntactic, with little reference to abstract notions. If the characterisations are in the form of natural deduction proof systems, they can be as clear and understandable as such proof systems are for describing conventional logics (see Gentzen [36] or Sundholm [71]).

Finally, characterising proof systems can be used directly to build systems for verifying correctness and termination properties of logic programs [5]. Schemes for proving properties of programs [14, 30] are related to the proof-theoretic tradition; they may be seen as "axiomatic" semantics (to use Stoy's [70] terminology) for logic programming.

2.2. Operational Semantics

The innovations of the logic programming paradigm lie to a large extent in its operational semantics. From a purely algorithmic viewpoint, a major advantage of logic programming for certain tasks is that the description of the solution can be expressed directly, while details of the control of *search* for the solution do not appear explicitly in the program. This is not to say that programmers do not need to be *aware* of the search strategy, however; if they are to write programs which are efficient and correct, they must know how the computer executes them. This is where the operational semantics can help.

Traditionally, operational semantics are given by some variant of SLD-resolution, which is in turn a specialisation of Robinson's resolution strategy [66]. SLD-resolution is sound and complete with respect to the model theory: whenever a query is satisfiable, it will find a solution, and it will never give a wrong solution. But SLD-resolution is nondeterministic in the sense that there may be more than one direction to proceed to find a proof of a given query. So to implement SLD-resolution completely, we need some kind of breadth-first search of the search space; but breadth-first search can be very inefficient, and for a number of reasons which I will discuss later, very few practical systems implement it.

The approach of most implementers of Prolog and other logic programming languages has been to implement SLD-resolution only partially and incompletely, or even unsoundly. The "occurs check" in the unification algorithm is often done away with, even though this results in occasional wrong solutions; and a sequential, left-to-right, depth-first search rule is often used to search the solution space, even though this does not find all solutions.

This sequential strategy has a fairly simple operational semantics, easily characterisable within the framework of SLD-resolution. But because it is not complete, there are queries which succeed, or fail, in full SLD-resolution which diverge (fail to terminate either way) in the sequential version. The loss of completeness is not felt very acutely by programmers, but the theoretical tradition has continued to study mostly the nondeterministic SLD-resolution and its model theory.

2.3. Declarative Semantics Revisited

How does this incompleteness of sequential Prolog reflect upon the declarative semantics of logic programming? The converse of this incompleteness is that the least-model and fixpoint semantics do not characterise sequential Prolog precisely: the set of successful queries in sequential Prolog is a subset of the set of satisfiable queries in the least model semantics. So there seems to be a split between theory and practice in logic programming, in which the theory is mostly about parallel systems and the practice mostly about sequential systems. To regain the original goals of the logic programming paradigm – practical programming languages based on logic – it seems that we have to either abandon the practical systems, or to give an abstract, declarative semantics for sequential Prolog.

The latter alternative seems to be desirable, but very little work has been done in this area. What has been done consists mostly of denotational semantics [48, 12, 57]. Denotational semantics characterises well the set of successful and failing queries, but it does so in a functional, non-logical manner. This is discouraging, because if we take a semantics as being a reflection of the intended paradigm, it suggests that practical logic programming is not "logical" at all, but a logical-looking variant of functional programming.

The main goal of this thesis is to give a declarative semantics of sequential logic programming, but to do so in a way which shows the language's clear connections with logic. In doing so, I hope to achieve a view of logic programming in which both the parallel and the sequential versions of the language fit equally well into an overall operational and declarative framework.

3. The Approach and Scope of This Thesis

This thesis follows the usual pattern of giving an operational semantics and a logical characterisation for logic programming languages, and proving equivalences between them.

I concentrate on studying the behaviour of the logical connectives in various logic programming systems, and in particular the behaviour of "and" and "or". I am specifically not concerned with other issues of incompleteness or unsoundness in logic programming implementations, such as the occurs check. I deal with a very simple language equivalent to Horn clauses – one which has no negation or cut, for instance – although I do suggest ways in which the language might be extended.

In the first technical chapter, Chapter 2, I give a definition of a very general operational semantics for this logic programming language. The operational semantics, SOS, is in the form of a formal tree-rewriting system or formal abstract machine. The basic operational semantics is one for a parallel-and, parallel-or system; a simple restriction on the application of the transition rules leads to a sequential-and system, and another, similar restriction leads to a sequential-or system. (Both restrictions together give the common "sequential Prolog" system.) I use SOS rather than the traditional SLD-resolution because it allows us to describe these various control strategies, including the failure-and-backtrack behaviour of sequential Prolog, within the formal system.

In Chapter 2, I also give several more compositional variants of SOS, which allow us to see more clearly some of the higher-level properties of computation in SOS. The chapter ends with a classification of the queries which succeed and fail with the four major control strategies (sequential or parallel "and", sequential or parallel "or").

In Chapters 3 and 4, I present the declarative semantics, which follow the proof-theoretic tradition mentioned above. The semantics take the form of sequent calculi. The elements of sequents in the calculus are *assertions*, which are expressions built up from *signed formulae* by the connectives of classical logic. Signed formulae, in turn, are essentially logic programming goal formulae enclosed by the sign S (for success) or F (for failure). The sequent calculi therefore retain a strong logical flavour.

The calculi in the two chapters share a set of rules called LKE. LKE is basically a Gentzen-style sequent calculus for classical first order logic with equality as syntactic identity. In Chapter 3, I concentrate on the problem of characterising queries which fail in parallel-and systems, and those which succeed in parallel-or systems; LKE is augmented by a set of simple logical axioms which describe the success and failure behaviour of queries under these assumptions. I prove the soundness of all the rules, and various completeness results about useful classes of sequents. One such completeness result is that if a query $\mathbf{A}$ succeeds (resp. fails), the sequent $[\rightarrow S(\exists[\mathbf{A}])]$ (resp. $[\rightarrow F(\exists[\mathbf{A}])]$) is derivable, where $\exists[\mathbf{A}]$ is the existential closure of $\mathbf{A}$. This amounts to a precise and logical characterisation of the sets of successful and failing queries.

In Chapter 4, on the other hand, I concentrate on characterising queries which succeed or fail in sequential-and, sequential-or systems. There is a similar set of axioms which correspond to this assumption; these axioms are made simple and compositional by the introduction of the notion of *disjunctive unfolding* of a formula. I prove similar soundness and completeness results about this calculus.

In addition to being able to prove assertions about the success and failure of individual queries, the sequent calculi are able to prove much more general properties of programs – such as the disjunctions, negations, and universal generalisations of such assertions. They therefore have important practical applications in software engineering: they can act as a basis for practical systems for proving properties of logic programs, such as proving that a program meets its specification.

There are limitations to how complete a finitary sequent calculus can be for this purpose, however. In Chapter 5, I explore this question of incompleteness. I give incompleteness results based on the Halting Problem and Gödel's incompleteness theorem to define some of the boundaries of the proof-theoretic approach. However, I also give some ways in which we can partially deal with this incompleteness: infinitary rules (a standard technique from logics of programs) and induction rules (which are very useful for practical program proving).

Finally, I discuss the import of the results and the directions that future research in this area could take in Chapter 6, and I give an Appendix with some examples of computations and derivations. There is an Index of Definitions at the end of the thesis which contains entries for all the formal, numbered definitions.

4. Definitional Preliminaries

Definition 4.1 A *first-order language* $\mathcal{L}$ consists of a set $\mathcal{X}(\mathcal{L})$ of variable names, a finite set $\mathcal{F}(\mathcal{L})$ of function symbols $\mathbf{f}_i$ each with an associated arity $n_i \geq 0$, and a set $\mathcal{P}(\mathcal{L})$ of predicate names $\mathbf{P}_j$ each with an associated arity $m_j \geq 0$.

The *terms* of a language $\mathcal{L}$ are inductively defined as follows: every variable of $\mathcal{L}$ is a term, and every expression $\mathbf{f}(\mathbf{t}_1, \ldots, \mathbf{t}_n)$, where $\mathbf{f}$ is a function symbol of arity n and $\mathbf{t}_1, \ldots, \mathbf{t}_n$ are terms, is a term; nothing else is a term. Nullary function symbol applications $\mathbf{f}()$ are often written as simply $\mathbf{f}$.

Following Miller and Nadathur [55], I will define the class of "goal formulae" as a restricted class of first order formulae built up from predicate applications using only the connectives "and", "or", and "there exists".

Definition 4.2 A *goal formula* in a first-order language $\mathcal{L}$ with a binary equality predicate $=$ is an expression which meets the following BNF syntax:

$$\mathbf{G} ::= \mathbf{s} = \mathbf{t} \;\mid\; \mathbf{P}(\mathbf{t}_1, \ldots, \mathbf{t}_n) \;\mid\; \mathbf{G}_1 \& \mathbf{G}_2 \;\mid\; \mathbf{G}_1 \vee \mathbf{G}_2 \;\mid\; \exists \mathbf{x}\, \mathbf{G}$$

where $\mathbf{s}$, $\mathbf{t}$, and the $\mathbf{t}_i$'s are all terms of $\mathcal{L}$, $\mathbf{P}$ is a predicate name of $\mathcal{L}$ of arity n, and $\mathbf{x}$ is a variable name of $\mathcal{L}$.

The class of goal formulae of $\mathcal{L}$ is thus a subclass of the class of formulae of $\mathcal{L}$. I will treat the word "query" as a synonym for "goal formula"; but I will use the former when we want to refer to a formula, possibly having free variables, for which we ask a logic programming system to find a satisfying substitution.

In the traditional approach to logic programming, used to describe Prolog and similar languages, programs are defined as sets of Horn clauses. Because I wish to compare logic programming systems directly with proof systems, I adopt a form of predicate definition which looks more like the completion of a predicate [21].

Definition 4.3 A *predicate definition* in $\mathcal{L}$ (defining the predicate $\mathbf{P}$) is an expression of the form

$$\mathbf{P}(\mathbf{x}_1, \mathbf{x}_2, \ldots, \mathbf{x}_n) \;\leftrightarrow\; \mathbf{A}$$

where the left- and right-hand sides of the $\leftrightarrow$ are goal formulae in $\mathcal{L}$, the $\mathbf{x}_i$'s are distinct, and the right-hand side contains no free variables not in $\{\mathbf{x}_1, \mathbf{x}_2, \ldots, \mathbf{x}_n\}$.

Definition 4.4 A *program* in $\mathcal{L}$ is a finite set of predicate definitions in which all names of predicates being defined are distinct.

This form is no loss or gain of power over the clausal form, but it makes connectives explicit and allows us to examine their effect and processing directly. To get a program of this form from a Horn clause program, we need only take the completion of the program [21]. Example: in a language with a binary function symbol $[\_|\_]$ of list formation, the standard "member" predicate Mem might be defined as follows:

$$Mem(x,l) \leftrightarrow \exists h\, \exists t\, (l = [h|t] \& (x = h \vee Mem(x,t)))$$

We will generally want to interpret a query **A** given to a logic programming system as a request to prove the existential closure of **A**. Since the logic we use will turn out to be constructive, this is the same as a request to find a satisfying substitution for **A**; the existential-closure view will just facilitate the comparison with the proof theory.

Definition 4.5 The *existential closure* of a formula **A**, in symbols $\exists[\mathbf{A}]$, is the formula $\exists \mathbf{x}_1 \ldots \exists \mathbf{x}_n \mathbf{A}$, where $\mathbf{x}_1 \ldots \mathbf{x}_n$ are all the free variables of **A**.

In the sequel we will assume the existence of some fixed first-order language $\mathcal{L}$ with equality $=$ as the language of all programs. We will further assume that $\mathcal{L}$ generates at least two closed terms. (This is not really a restriction for most practical applications.) We will write these closed terms as 0 and 1, and define the formula *true* as an abbreviation for $0 = 0$, and *false* as an abbreviation for $0 = 1$.

In most of what follows, we will also assume the existence of at least one non-nullary operation symbol; that is, we will assume that the language has an infinite number of closed terms. This is a reasonable assumption for most logic programming applications, but not so for the area of logic databases, where there may be only a finite number of data elements in the domain of discourse. I will point out the use of the assumption of an infinite domain whenever it is used, and discuss the implications of this.

Other notation is as follows. **A**, **B**, **C**, **D** are metavariables standing for goal formulae; **P**, **Q**, and **R** stand for predicate names; **r**, **s**, and **t** stand for terms; and **x**, **y**, and **z** stand for variables.

θ and ρ stand for substitutions. $\mathbf{A}\theta$ stands for the application of θ to **A** (where all substitutions of terms for variables take place simultaneously, and may involve renaming to avoid capture of free variables); similarly $\mathbf{t}\theta$ stands for θ applied to the term **t**. $[\mathbf{x} := \mathbf{t}]$ is the substitution which maps only **x** to **t**.

I use the notation $\mathbf{A}(\mathbf{s})$ and then later $\mathbf{A}(\mathbf{t})$ to mean $\mathbf{A}[\mathbf{x} := \mathbf{s}]$ and then later $\mathbf{A}[\mathbf{x} := \mathbf{t}]$, for some given formula **A** with some given variable **x** free. ($\mathbf{A}(\mathbf{x})$ should not be confused with $\mathbf{P}(\mathbf{x})$, which is an application of predicate **P** to variable **x**.) Similarly I use $\mathbf{r}[\mathbf{s} := \mathbf{t}]$, $\mathbf{r}(\mathbf{s})$, $\mathbf{r}(\mathbf{t})$.

Chapter 2

Operational Semantics

Operational (or "procedural") semantics, as I mentioned in the Introduction, are used to provide characterisations of programming languages which meet certain "computational" criteria: giving a detailed description of the language for implementation purposes, and giving a computational model to which programmers can refer.

For logic programming, operational semantics are particularly important because it is in them that the innovations of logic programming lie. The notions of resolution and unification are not immediately apparent; unification, though defined by Herbrand in his thesis [44], was virtually ignored until Prawitz's work [62], and resolution was not defined until 1965 [66]. These notions must be explained within the context of a full description of the computational model of the language.

If we want to do such things as soundness and completeness proofs, or indeed any formal comparison of the operational semantics to other characterisations of the language, the operational semantics must also be mathematically precise – for instance, in the form of a formal system. (Plotkin [58] has explored the idea of structured operational semantics in detail, and gives a taxonomy to which I will refer in this chapter.) SLD-resolution [49], SLDNF-resolution [50], and the operational semantics in this chapter are just a few examples of formal operational semantics for logic programming. Other examples include Voda's tree-rewriting system [76], Deransart and Ferrand's [29] and Börger's [13] standardisation efforts, and the abstract computation engines for Andorra Prolog [43] and the "Pure Logic Language", PLL [10, 52]. The operational semantics which is closest to the one in this chapter is perhaps that in de Bruin and Vink's continuation semantics paper [26].

SLD-resolution is an adequate operational semantics for logic programming, but one not quite suited to our purposes. SLD-resolution is centred around the idea of a program as a set or sequence of Horn clauses, which in turn are sets or sequences of literals. In our view of a program as a set of definitions of predicates by goal-formula bodies, we must give an operational semantics which manipulates goal formulae as its basic units. In the various operational semantics to be given in this chapter, each transition rule concerns itself with a single form of goal formula (disjunction, conjunction, predicate call and so on), in keeping with our study of how systems treat the various connectives. In addition, the nature of SLD-resolution requires us to use rules external to the operational semantics ("subgoal selection rules" and "search rules") to characterise such things as backtracking in sequential-or systems; such notions are entirely integrated into the operational semantics in this chapter.

In this chapter, I first discuss the various control disciplines and their uses, and then give the parallel-and, parallel-or operational semantics SOS ("stack of stacks"), which will act as a reference point throughout the rest of the thesis. Sequential-and and sequential-or systems are simple variants of SOS, and have certain completeness properties with respect to SOS; these I describe next. I also give some more compositional variants of SOS, which will be useful in later chapters for proving theorems. I give some somewhat technical lemmas about the behaviour of existential quantifiers, which will be used frequently in later chapters. The chapter ends with a summary of the classification of all queries according as if they succeed, fail, or diverge in the various control disciplines described in this chapter.

1. Control Disciplines and their Uses

This chapter gives operational semantics for several different control disciplines. It will therefore be useful to review why we want to do this, and what the various control disciplines are useful for.

The implementation of a logic programming system involves choices about how *complete* it is going to be. When we give a query formula **A** with free variables to the system, we want it to find a substitution θ such that $\mathbf{A}\theta$ is true, given the standard definition of logical truth and the predicate definitions in the program. The ideal – a complete system – is a system which can find such substitution whenever it exists.

Unfortunately, this ideal cannot be realised without there being some form of parallelism in the interpreter – that is, some coprocessing, timesharing, or breadth-first search. The crucial problems centre around the two binary connectives, the conjunction & and the disjunction $\vee$. Say that the interpreter processes queries of the form **B&C** by first processing **B** and then processing **C**. Then, although a query such as **B**&$false$ has no solution, if the processing of **B** causes the interpreter to go into an infinite loop, then the interpreter will never discover that it has no solution: the interpreter will be incomplete for failure. Similarly, interpreters which process disjunctions in this sequential manner will be incomplete for success, never finding solutions to some queries which have solutions.

Nevertheless, this "sequential" control discipline for one or both of the binary connectives is very common in many logic programming systems, and is likely to remain so [31]. Sequential "and" and "or" are easy to implement in a simple stack-based interpreter, and yield an execution model, based on sequential execution and backtrack, which makes it relatively easy to follow the execution of a program for debugging purposes. In contrast, giving an efficient implementation of a language with parallel "and" and "or" involves optimising such things as resource sharing and process switching. It is also more difficult to debug a program when there are several things going on at once, as in parallel programs, rather than just one stream of computation. Added to these technical considerations is the empirical observation that the loss of completeness in sequential systems appears to be relatively easy for programmers to work around.

Sequential "and" and "or" are, therefore, both used in most commercial Prologs and other logic programming languages. Parallel "and" and "or" [24, 23, 67] are the exception, rather than the rule, and are generally used only when there is some particular application that works better with them. Parallel "or" is useful for problems with a complex logical structure, in which it is unclear which of several alternatives will lead to a solution. Since parallel-or systems are complete for successful queries (as we shall see below), one use of such systems might be as execution engines for executing Horn clause specifications, because such specifications are intended to be very high-level and free from operational considerations.

Parallel "and" systems are useful for problems which can benefit from the more traditional parallelisation of computation, done to make independent computations more efficient. They are also useful for doing programming in which predicate calls joined by a conjunction represent communicating agents, such as sequential processes, coroutines, or objects [68, 67].

In some systems with parallel connectives [76], the sequential versions of these connectives are also available (usually distinguished by a different syntax). Here, I will be simplifying the situation and considering only systems in which there is one kind of each connective; there is one conjunction, which is either always parallel or always sequential, and similarly one disjunction. I do this mainly to make the operational semantics simpler and thus more amenable to analysis.

2. Stack-of-Stacks Operational Semantics: SOS

The first operational semantics I will describe will be a formalisation of the common "stack of stacks" implementation of Prolog. It is called the stack of stacks technique because the machine state is given by a "backtrack stack" whose elements are "closures" containing "goal stacks".

In Plotkin's taxonomy [58], this would be a "multi-step" system; the rules for the formal system define one step in a computation, and we are more interested in the transitive closure of the relation thus defined. Later we will see "single-step" systems, in which the relation is between one state and the final state of the entire computation.

I use the word "stack" to emphasise the analogy of certain expressions with the stack data structure known to computer programmers, because it is this data structure that is used in many implementations. However, such implementations are sequential and deterministic, and we will be studying operational semantics which may be parallel and nondeterministic. Thus, something which is called a stack here might not always be operated on by the usual push, pop, and top operations on stacks, but also by the selection of an arbitrary element from the stack, or the replacement of an arbitrary element by 0 or more elements. I hope that the advantage of familiar terminology will outweigh the disadvantage of imprecise usage. I will point out the cases in which a stack really is behaving as a computer science stack.

2.1. Definitions and Rules

Definition 2.1 A *goal stack* is just a sequence of formulae. We will generally use α, possibly subscripted, to stand for an arbitrary goal stack. We will write the concatenation of two goal stacks α_1 and α_2 as α_1, α_2. We will sometimes refer to the formulae in a goal stack as *subgoals*.

A *closure* is an expression $(\theta : \alpha)$, where α is a goal stack and θ is a substitution. (In practice, θ will be some syntactic representation of a substitution on a finite number of variables.)

A *backtrack stack* is a sequence of closures. We will generally use β, possibly subscripted, to stand for an arbitrary backtrack stack. We will write the concatenation of

1. &:
   $\beta_1; (\theta : \alpha_1, (\mathbf{B} \& \mathbf{C}), \alpha_2); \beta_2 \stackrel{\text{SOS}}{\Rightarrow} \beta_1; (\theta : \alpha_1, \mathbf{B}, \mathbf{C}, \alpha_2); \beta_2$

2. $\vee$:
   $\beta_1; (\theta : \alpha_1, (\mathbf{B} \vee \mathbf{C}), \alpha_2); \beta_2 \stackrel{\text{SOS}}{\Rightarrow} \beta_1; (\theta : \alpha_1, \mathbf{B}, \alpha_2); (\theta : \alpha_1, \mathbf{C}, \alpha_2); \beta_2$

3. $\exists$:
   $\beta_1; (\theta : \alpha_1, (\exists \mathbf{x} \mathbf{B}), \alpha_2); \beta_2 \stackrel{\text{SOS}}{\Rightarrow} \beta_1; (\theta : \alpha_1, \mathbf{B}[\mathbf{x} := \mathbf{x}'], \alpha_2); \beta_2$
   where $\mathbf{x}'$ is some variable not appearing free to the left of the arrow

4. Defined predicates:
   $\beta_1; (\theta : \alpha_1, \mathbf{P}(\mathbf{t}_1, \ldots, \mathbf{t}_n), \alpha_2); \beta_2 \stackrel{\text{SOS}}{\Rightarrow} \beta_1; (\theta : \alpha_1, \mathbf{A}(\mathbf{t}_1, \ldots, \mathbf{t}_n), \alpha_2); \beta_2$
   where Π contains the definition $(\mathbf{P}(\mathbf{x}_1, \ldots, \mathbf{x}_n) \leftrightarrow \mathbf{A}(\mathbf{x}_1, \ldots, \mathbf{x}_n))$

5. Unification, success:
   $\beta_1; (\theta : \alpha_1, \mathbf{s} = \mathbf{t}, \alpha_2); \beta_2 \stackrel{\text{SOS}}{\Rightarrow} \beta_1; (\theta\theta' : \alpha_1, \alpha_2); \beta_2$
   where θ' is the mgu of $\mathbf{s}\theta$ and $\mathbf{t}\theta$

6. Unification, failure:
   $\beta_1; (\theta : \alpha_1, \mathbf{s} = \mathbf{t}, \alpha_2); \beta_2 \stackrel{\text{SOS}}{\Rightarrow} \beta_1; \beta_2$
   where $\mathbf{s}\theta$ and $\mathbf{t}\theta$ do not unify

Figure 2.1. Rules for the operational semantics SOS.

two backtrack stacks β_1 and β_2 as $\beta_1; \beta_2$.
ϵ will represent the empty goal stack or backtrack stack (its use will be non-ambiguous).

Logically, a backtrack stack

$$(\theta_1 : \mathbf{A}_{11}, \ldots, \mathbf{A}_{1n_1}); \ldots; (\theta_m : \mathbf{A}_{m1}, \ldots, \mathbf{A}_{mn_m})$$

represents the formula

$$(\mathbf{A}_{11}\theta_1 \& \ldots \& \mathbf{A}_{1n_1}\theta_1 \& true) \vee \ldots \vee (\mathbf{A}_{m1}\theta_m \& \ldots \& \mathbf{A}_{mn_m}\theta_m \& true) \vee false$$

for which we are trying to find a satisfying substitution. Thus the elements of a goal stack represent subgoals, all of which are to be solved in the context of the substitution in their closure; and the elements of a backtrack stack represent different alternatives, any one of which may yield a solution.

There will be one operational semantics, called SOS_Π, corresponding to each program Π. (Since the particular program being considered will usually not be important, we will usually drop the subscript.) SOS is a rewriting system which consists of rules for a binary relation $\stackrel{\text{SOS}}{\Rightarrow}$ between backtrack stacks, and a definition of which backtrack stacks are to be considered "success states" and "failure states".

The rewriting rules of SOS are in Figure 2.1. The success states of SOS are all backtrack stacks of the form

$$\beta_1; (\theta : \epsilon); \beta_2$$

that is, all backtrack stacks containing a closure with an empty goal stack. The single failure state of SOS is ϵ, the empty backtrack stack.

To execute a particular goal formula **A** in this interpreter, we form the backtrack stack consisting of the single closure $(() : \mathbf{A})$, where $()$ is the empty substitution. We then repeatedly apply appropriate transitions. If we reach a failure state, we conclude that the query is unsatisfiable; if we reach a success state $\beta_1; (\theta : \epsilon); \beta_2$, we conclude that θ is a satisfying substitution for **A**. Of course, for a given goal we might never reach a success or a failure state, due to repeated diverging applications of the defined predicate rule.

Definition 2.2 The relation $\stackrel{\text{SOS}*}{\Rightarrow}$ is the reflexive and transitive closure of the $\stackrel{\text{SOS}}{\Rightarrow}$ relation.

We say that a backtrack stack β *succeeds* if $\beta \stackrel{\text{SOS}*}{\Rightarrow} \beta'$, where β' is a success state.

We say that β *fails* if $\beta \stackrel{\text{SOS}*}{\Rightarrow} \epsilon$.

We say that β *diverges* if it neither succeeds nor fails.

We say that a query formula **A** succeeds (fails, diverges) if the backtrack stack $(() : \mathbf{A})$ succeeds (fails, diverges), where $()$ is the empty substitution.

We say that SOS describes a "parallel and" discipline because each conjunction in a backtrack stack is processed by splitting it into its subformulae, after which point the computational rules can operate on either subformula. We say that it describes a "parallel or" discipline for similar reasons.

2.2. Properties of SOS

We will leave discussion of the logical properties of this operational semantics to later chapters, and here will concentrate on the combinatorial, operational properties of SOS. To begin, SOS has the Church-Rosser property that any two computations diverging from the same point can converge again (up to a natural equivalence).

We must begin by proving the Church-Rosser property of a slightly weaker system, namely the system SOS without the Defined Predicate rule. The notion of equivalence is the same.

Definition 2.3 Two backtrack stacks β_1, β_2 are *renaming-permutation-equivalent* if they are identical up to a (closure-wise) renaming of variables and a permutation of closures.

Let fSOS be the operational semantics SOS without the Defined Predicate rule.

Theorem 2.4 (Church-Rosser Property of fSOS)
1. (Diamond property.) If $\beta \stackrel{\text{fSOS}}{\Rightarrow} \beta_1$ and $\beta \stackrel{\text{fSOS}}{\Rightarrow} \beta_2$, then there is a β' such that $\beta \stackrel{\text{fSOS}*}{\Rightarrow} \beta_1$ and $\beta \stackrel{\text{fSOS}*}{\Rightarrow} \beta_2$, up to renaming-permutation equivalence.
2. (Strong normalisation.) There is no infinite computation sequence in fSOS, and every computation sequence can be extended to reach a backtrack stack for which no further transitions are possible.
3. (Church-Rosser property.) If $\beta \stackrel{\text{fSOS}*}{\Rightarrow} \beta_1$ and $\beta \stackrel{\text{fSOS}*}{\Rightarrow} \beta_2$, then there is a β' such that $\beta_1 \stackrel{\text{fSOS}*}{\Rightarrow} \beta'$ and $\beta_2 \stackrel{\text{fSOS}*}{\Rightarrow} \beta'$.

Proof : (1.) By case analysis. If the two computations select the same subgoal in the same closure, then β_1 and β_2 are already renaming-permutation-equivalent. Otherwise, a different subgoal, possibly in different closures, has been selected for processing. The cases are on the form of the subgoals selected.

If both subgoals are existential formulae, then the computations can converge in one step. If both computations selected the same new variable, then the convergence is only up to a renaming of the new variables.

Otherwise, if each subgoal is in a different closure, then the computations can converge identically in one step, because nothing that goes on in one closure can affect others.

Otherwise, both subgoals are in the same closure, but are not both existentials. If both are disjunctions, then the computations can converge in two steps, by each branch performing a Disjunction step on the two copies of the other disjunction. The convergence here is only up to a permutation of the closures: if the two disjunctions were $\mathbf{A} \vee \mathbf{B}$ and $\mathbf{C} \vee \mathbf{D}$, then β_1 will contain closures containing (in order) $\mathbf{A} \ldots \mathbf{C}, \mathbf{A} \ldots \mathbf{D}, \mathbf{B} \ldots \mathbf{C}$, and $\mathbf{B} \ldots \mathbf{D}$, whereas β_2 will contain closures containing (in order) $\mathbf{A} \ldots \mathbf{C}, \mathbf{B} \ldots \mathbf{C}, \mathbf{A} \ldots \mathbf{D}$, and $\mathbf{B} \ldots \mathbf{D}$.

Otherwise, if both subgoals are equalities, then we can consider without loss of generality the case where the first computation is $(\theta : \mathbf{s}_1 = \mathbf{t}_1, \mathbf{s}_2 = \mathbf{t}_2) \stackrel{\text{fSOS}}{\Rightarrow} (\theta\theta_1 : \mathbf{s}_2 = \mathbf{t}_2)$ and the second computation is $(\theta : \mathbf{s}_1 = \mathbf{t}_1, \mathbf{s}_2 = \mathbf{t}_2) \stackrel{\text{fSOS}}{\Rightarrow} (\theta\theta_2 : \mathbf{s}_1 = \mathbf{t}_1)$. There are two subcases.

- There is no θ'_1 such that $\mathbf{s}_2\theta\theta_1\theta'_1 \equiv \mathbf{t}_2\theta\theta_1\theta'_1$. In this case the first computation ends in failure. Now, if there were a θ'_2 such that $\mathbf{s}_1\theta\theta_2\theta'_2 \equiv \mathbf{t}_1\theta\theta_2\theta'_2$, then (by the properties of mgu on θ_1, the mgu of $\mathbf{s}_1\theta$ and $\mathbf{t}_1\theta$) there would be a θ'_1 such that $\theta\theta_2\theta'_2 \equiv \theta\theta_1\theta'_1$. But since $\mathbf{s}_2\theta\theta_2\theta'_2 \equiv \mathbf{t}_2\theta\theta_2\theta'_2$, we have that $\mathbf{s}_2\theta\theta_1\theta'_1 \equiv \mathbf{t}_2\theta\theta_1\theta'_1$; so θ'_1 would have the property that we started out by assuming that no substitution could have. There is therefore no such θ'_2, and the second computation fails as well.

- There is a θ'_1 such that $\mathbf{s}_2\theta\theta_1\theta'_1 \equiv \mathbf{t}_2\theta\theta_1\theta'_1$. In this case (by the properties of mgu on θ_2), there is also a θ'_2 such that $\theta\theta_1\theta'_1 \equiv \theta\theta_2\theta'_2$; therefore the second computation performs a Unification step, resulting in an identical goal stack (up to renaming of variables, since mgu's are unique up to renaming of variables).

Otherwise, both subgoals are in the same closure, but are not both existentials, disjunctions, or equalities. If one of the subgoals is a disjunction, then the computations can converge in two steps on the disjunction branch (similar steps on the two copies of the other subgoal), and one step on the other branch.

In all other cases (one or both subgoals are conjunctions, or one is an equality and the other is an existential), the computation of each subgoal does not interfere with that of the other, so the computations can converge in one step.

(2.) Let the ordinal measure $m(C)$ of a closure C be $j \cdot 2^k$, where j is the number of connectives and equality formulae in C, and k is the number of disjunctions in C. Let the measure $m(\beta)$ of a backtrack stack β be the sum of the measures of its closures. Then every transition in fSOS lowers the measure of the backtrack stack, since every transition eliminates at least one connective or equality formula except the $\vee$ rule, which changes the measure from $j \cdot 2^k$ to $2((j-1) \cdot 2^{k-1}) = (j-1) \cdot 2^k$.

Thus, by induction, no infinite computation sequence is possible. The only backtrack stacks in which no transitions are possible are ones containing only predicate calls (ones with measure 0). We say that these backtrack stacks are in *normal form*. Since fSOS computation steps can be performed on any backtrack stack not in normal form, every computation can be extended to reach a backtrack stack in normal form.

(3.) (A variant of Newman's Lemma [11].) From (1) and (2). Call a backtrack stack from which two distinct normal forms are computable *ambiguous*. We will prove by reductio ad absurdum that there are no ambiguous backtrack stacks.

Assume that there is an ambiguous backtrack stack β, of measure m; in other words, that $\beta \overset{\text{fSOS}*}{\Rightarrow} \beta_1$, $\beta \overset{\text{fSOS}*}{\Rightarrow} \beta_2$, and β_1 and β_2 are in normal form and not renaming-permutation equivalent. These computations must consist of at least one step each. If the first step in the two computations is the same, then there is an ambiguous backtrack stack with measure less than m (namely, the backtrack stack arrived at after this first step).

Otherwise, the two computations make a first step to β_1' and β_2', respectively; by the Diamond property, there are computations leading from both β_1' and β_2' to some β'. Now say that there is a computation leading from β' to some normal form β''. Either β'' is equivalent to β_1, in which case it is not equivalent to β_2, in which case β_1' is ambiguous; or β'' is equivalent to β_2, in which case it is not equivalent to β_1, in which case β_2' is ambiguous; or β'' is equivalent to neither, in which case both β_1' and β_2' are ambiguous. In any case, there is an ambiguous backtrack stack of lower measure than β. By induction, therefore, there is an ambiguous backtrack stack of measure 0; but this is impossible, since backtrack stacks of measure 0 are in normal form.

Thus, the normal form of a backtrack stack β is unique; every computation proceeding from β can be extended to this unique normal form; and thus if $\beta \overset{\text{fSOS}*}{\Rightarrow} \beta_1$ and $\beta \overset{\text{fSOS}*}{\Rightarrow} \beta_2$, then there is a β' (namely, the unique normal form) such that $\beta \overset{\text{fSOS}*}{\Rightarrow} \beta_1$ and $\beta \overset{\text{fSOS}*}{\Rightarrow} \beta_2$. □

To obtain the analogous result about SOS, we need to separate the steps of an SOS computation into the predicate "unfoldings" and the connective steps. The following notion, which will also be necessary in later proof-theoretic characterisations, will help to capture this.

Definition 2.5 β' is a *predicate 1-unfolding* of a backtrack stack β if it is β with one predicate application subformula $\mathbf{P}(\mathbf{t}_1, \ldots, \mathbf{t}_n)$ replaced by $\mathbf{A}(\mathbf{t}_1, \ldots, \mathbf{t}_n)$, where $\mathbf{P}(\mathbf{x}_1, \ldots, \mathbf{x}_n) \leftrightarrow \mathbf{A}(\mathbf{x}_1, \ldots, \mathbf{x}_n)$ is in the program Π.

β' is a *predicate unfolding* of a backtrack stack β if it is β with 0 or more successive predicate 1-unfoldings applied to it.

Theorem 2.6 (Church-Rosser Property of SOS) *If $\beta \overset{\text{SOS}*}{\Rightarrow} \beta_1$ and $\beta \overset{\text{SOS}*}{\Rightarrow} \beta_2$, then there is a β' such that $\beta_1 \overset{\text{SOS}*}{\Rightarrow} \beta'$ and $\beta_2 \overset{\text{SOS}*}{\Rightarrow} \beta'$.*

Proof : First of all, note that there are predicate unfoldings β^+ of β, β_1^+ of β_1, and β_2^+ of β_2, such that $\beta^+ \overset{\text{fSOS}*}{\Rightarrow} \beta_1^+$ and $\beta^+ \overset{\text{fSOS}*}{\Rightarrow} \beta_2^+$: we can identify in β the predicate application subformula which gets unfolded first in the computation of β_1 and perform a predicate 1-unfolding on β for that, and so on for the other predicate steps in the computations of β_1 and β_2. The fSOS computations will then be just the steps in the SOS computations other than the predicate steps; the unfoldings will not interfere with these steps. β_1^+ might not be identical to β_1 because it will have some predicates unfolded to account for the steps toward β_2, or some unfolded subformulae duplicated due to the $\vee$ rule.

Now, from the Strong Normalisation and Church-Rosser properties of fSOS, we know that there is a β' in normal form such that $\beta_1^+ \stackrel{fSOS*}{\Rightarrow} \beta'$ and $\beta_2^+ \stackrel{fSOS*}{\Rightarrow} \beta'$. β' is thus accessible from β_1 and β_2 by a series of predicate unfoldings followed by a series of fSOS steps. However, we can form an SOS-computation of β' from β_1 by inserting Defined Predicate steps corresponding to each predicate unfolding, at the points where each instance of the predicate call in question becomes a top-level element of a backtrack stack. We can do the same to derive an SOS-computation of β' from β_2. □

This theorem has some interesting consequences. The most important of these are the following.

Corollary 2.7 If any computation of β reaches the failure state, then no computation of β can reach a success state.

Proof : By the theorem, if this were possible, then the two computations could be extended to meet (up to renaming-permutation equivalence). But there is no computation proceeding from the failure state; and no computation proceeding from a success state (which has one closure to which no rules apply) can reach a failure state (which has no closures). □

This means that a query cannot both succeed and fail; the set of succeeding backtrack stacks and the set of failing backtrack stacks are disjoint. (Below, we will study further some of the structure of these two sets.)

Corollary 2.8 If a computation of β reaches a success state β' whose successful closure is $(\theta : \epsilon)$, then every computation of β can reach such a success state (up to renaming-disjunction equivalence).

Proof : Every backtrack stack which is a descendent of β' will contain $(\theta : \epsilon)$ as a closure, because no rules will eliminate it. By the Church-Rosser property, any computation can reach a descendent of β'. □

This means that if one solution is found, this does not preclude the finding of other solutions. Thus we can characterise the behaviour of a goal stack by giving the set of substitutions which can appear as solutions in successful computations (failing stacks taking the empty set).

2.3. Discussion

The major difference between SLD-resolution and SOS is that disjunctive information is made explicit. In SLD-resolution, each resolution step chooses one clause from the program; however, information about which clauses have been tried and which have yet to be tried is not explicit in the formal system. This means that information about how a particular system tries clauses must be represented outside the formal system (typically by a "search rule" in the search tree of candidate clauses [50]). In SOS, clause information corresponds to the placement of the halves of a disjunction on the backtrack stack. As we will see, this facilitates the definition of sequential computations as variants of the single formal system.

The disadvantages of this "multi-step" style of operational semantics, in general, are that it is not very compositional, and that (except for the sequential variant) it is non-deterministic and therefore not a detailed description of an implementation.

I say that it is not very compositional because transitions depend not on the structure of high-level elements of the formal system (backtrack stacks) but on the structure of fairly low-level ones (individual formulae within goal stacks). Each transition involves a change to what may be only a small part of the elements of the system. This makes SOS a fairly clumsy system for proof purposes, since a lot of manipulation of structure is required in proofs involving it. Later, we will see other operational semantics which are more compositional; these will help to make clear some of the higher-level properties of SOS computations, and we will sometimes use these systems in the later soundness and completeness proofs.

The nondeterminism of SOS (which it shares with SLD-resolution) is a practical problem, because although the nondeterminism is used to model parallelism, it is not clear how this parallelism is to be implemented. However, there are so many ways of implementing parallelism (explicit breadth-first search or dovetailing on a rule-by-rule basis, process creation on a timesharing machine, actual parallel computation by parallel processors, etc.) that perhaps this is better left up to the implementor's choice.

3. Sequential Variants of SOS

SOS is an operational semantics in which nondeterminism is used to model parallelism. If we imagine an implementation in which each formula in each goal stack is assigned a processor, then a computation step corresponds to one of the processors completing the task of transforming the backtrack stack based on the form of its formula. The nondeterminism in the choice of formula reflects the fact that any of the processors may happen to finish its task first.

Thus, we can model a lower degree of parallelism in the implementation by restricting the choice of subgoal to be processed. Restricting the choosable subgoals to those in the first closure means that when a disjunction $\mathbf{B} \vee \mathbf{C}$ causes the backtrack stack to be split by an application of the $\vee$ rule, we must finish processing of **B** before we can move on to **C**; the processing of the disjunction becomes sequential. Similarly, restricting the choosable subgoals to those on the top of their respective goal stacks means that in the processing of a conjunction **B**&**C**, the computation of **B** must finish before **C** can be processed.

3.1. Definitions and Rules

Definition 3.1 A computation $\beta \overset{\mathrm{SOS}*}{\Rightarrow} \beta'$ is *sequential-or* if the subgoal selected for processing at each step is in the leftmost closure of the backtrack stack.

A computation sequence $\beta \overset{\mathrm{SOS}*}{\Rightarrow} \beta'$ is *sequential-and* if the subgoal selected for processing at each step is the leftmost subgoal in its goal stack ("at the top of its goal stack").

A computation sequence is *sequential-both* if it is both sequential-or and sequential-and.

We will call SOS restricted to sequential-or computations SOS/so, and SOS restricted to sequential-and computations SOS/sa. We will call SOS restricted to sequential-both computations SOS/sao, or more simply SP (Sequential Prolog).

There is only one sequential-both computation sequence of a given backtrack stack; that is, the operational semantics SP is *monogenic.* (We ignore renaming of variables here, assuming that our system has a deterministic algorithm for selecting variable names in

1. &:
$(\theta : (\mathbf{B}\&\mathbf{C}), \alpha); \beta \stackrel{SP}{\Rightarrow} (\theta : \mathbf{B}, \mathbf{C}, \alpha); \beta$

2. $\vee$:
$(\theta : (\mathbf{B} \vee \mathbf{C}), \alpha); \beta \stackrel{SP}{\Rightarrow} (\theta : \mathbf{B}, \alpha); (\theta : \mathbf{C}, \alpha); \beta$

3. $\exists$:
$(\theta : (\exists \mathbf{x} \mathbf{B}), \alpha); \beta \stackrel{SP}{\Rightarrow} (\theta : \mathbf{B}[\mathbf{x} := \mathbf{x}'], \alpha); \beta$
where $\mathbf{x}'$ is some variable not appearing to the left of the arrow

4. Defined predicates:
$(\theta : \mathbf{P}(\mathbf{t}_1, \ldots, \mathbf{t}_n), \alpha); \beta \stackrel{SP}{\Rightarrow} (\theta : \mathbf{A}(\mathbf{t}_1, \ldots, \mathbf{t}_n), \alpha); \beta$
where Π contains the definition $(\mathbf{P}(\mathbf{x}_1, \ldots, \mathbf{x}_n) \leftrightarrow \mathbf{A}(\mathbf{x}_1, \ldots, \mathbf{x}_n))$

5. Unification, success:
$(\theta : \mathbf{s} = \mathbf{t}, \alpha); \beta \stackrel{SP}{\Rightarrow} (\theta\theta' : \alpha); \beta$
where θ' is the mgu of $\mathbf{s}\theta$ and $\mathbf{t}\theta$

6. Unification, failure:
$(\theta : \mathbf{s} = \mathbf{t}, \alpha); \beta \stackrel{SP}{\Rightarrow} \beta$
where $\mathbf{s}\theta$ and $\mathbf{t}\theta$ do not unify

Figure 2.2. The rules of the operational semantics SP.

the $\exists$ rule and for selecting an mgu in the unification algorithm.) In the case of sequential-both computations, the stacks really do behave as stacks, with the top of the stack to the left: nothing is relevant to the computation except the leftmost subgoal in the goal stack of the leftmost closure. Because only one choice of subgoal is possible, SP does not need to be implemented by more than one processor.

Sequential-both computations are the most practically important class of computations, because many logic programming interpreters use only the sequential strategy. Because we will want to study sequential-both computations in great detail later, it will be useful to set down the rules of SP explicitly.

The rules of SP are as in Figure 2.2. The success states of SP are the backtrack stacks of the form $(\theta : \epsilon); \beta$. The single failure state of SP is the empty backtrack stack, ϵ.

3.2. Completeness Properties of Sequential Computations

Theorem 3.2 (SOS-Failure Completeness of SOS/so) If β has a failing SOS-computation, then it has a failing sequential-or computation.

Proof: By induction on the length of the computation. Clearly a computation of zero steps is sequential-or. If the computation has one or more steps, then consider the first step in the failing computation which applies to the leftmost closure. If this is the first step of the computation, then by the induction hypothesis, the result holds.

Otherwise, the computation consists of an initial segment, the first step which applies to the leftmost closure, and a final segment. (There must be at least one step which applies to the leftmost closure, because the leftmost must fail.) We can form a new computation by taking β, performing the central step which replaces the leftmost closure C by a stack β'; appending to that the initial segment, with C replaced by β' everywhere; and appending to that the final segment. The computation consisting of the altered initial segment and the final segment has, by the induction hypothesis, a failing sequential-or computation; so the original stack β has a failing sequential-or computation. □

Example. Consider the following computation:

$$
\begin{aligned}
((): 0 = 1); ((): \exists x(x = 2 \& x = 3)) &\stackrel{\text{SOS}}{\Rightarrow} ((): 0 = 1); ((): x = 2 \& x = 3) \quad (\exists) \\
&\stackrel{\text{SOS}}{\Rightarrow} ((): 0 = 1); ((): x = 2, x = 3) \quad (\&) \\
&\stackrel{\text{SOS}}{\Rightarrow} ((): x = 2, x = 3) \quad \text{(Unif, fail)} \\
&\stackrel{\text{SOS}}{\Rightarrow} ([x := 3]: x = 2) \quad \text{(Unif, succ)} \\
&\stackrel{\text{SOS}}{\Rightarrow} \epsilon \quad \text{(Unif, fail)}
\end{aligned}
$$

This computation can be transformed into the following sequential-or computation:

$$
\begin{aligned}
((): 0 = 1); ((): \exists x(x = 2 \& x = 3)) &\stackrel{\text{SOS}}{\Rightarrow} ((): \exists x(x = 2 \& x = 3)) \quad \text{(Unif, fail)} \\
&\stackrel{\text{SOS}}{\Rightarrow} ((): x = 2 \& x = 3) \quad (\exists) \\
&\stackrel{\text{SOS}}{\Rightarrow} ((): x = 2, x = 3) \quad (\&) \\
&\stackrel{\text{SOS}}{\Rightarrow} ([x := 3]: x = 2) \quad \text{(Unif, succ)} \\
&\stackrel{\text{SOS}}{\Rightarrow} \epsilon \quad \text{(Unif, fail)}
\end{aligned}
$$

So failing SOS-computations have SOS/so-analogues. Failing SOS-computations do not necessarily have SOS/sa-analogues, however. Consider the infinitely-looping predicate *Loop*, defined by the predicate definition

$$Loop() \leftrightarrow Loop()$$

The query $Loop() \& false$ fails in SOS but diverges for SOS/sa. (Recall that $false$ is an abbreviation for $0 = 1$, where 0 and 1 are distinct closed terms.) However, there is an analogous relationship between sequential-and and sequential-both computations. This is not a straightforward consequence of the last theorem, because the set of failing computations of SOS/sa is a subset of that of SOS, and that of SP is a subset of that of SOS/so. However, the proof is very similar.

Theorem 3.3 (SOS/sa-Failure Completeness of SP) If β has a failing sequential-and computation, then it has a failing sequential-both computation.

Proof : As in the proof of the last theorem. □

The analogous property for success goes the other way: successful SOS-computations have sequential-and analogues, but not necessarily sequential-or analogues (the query $Loop() \lor true$ is a counterexample).

First, a technical lemma.

Lemma 3.4 (Independence of Closures for Success)
(1) The backtrack stack β succeeds in SOS iff some element of β (that is, some closure in β, taken as a singleton backtrack stack) succeeds in a smaller or equal number of steps. (2) The backtrack stack β succeeds in SOS/sa iff some element of β succeeds in SOS/sa in a smaller or equal number of steps.

Proof : (1, $\rightarrow$) By induction on the length of the computation. If β is a success state itself, then the result holds trivially. Otherwise, let $\beta \stackrel{SOS}{\Rightarrow} \beta'$ be the first step. By the induction hypothesis, one of the closures in β' succeeds. If this closure appears in β, then the result holds. Otherwise, it is the product of a computation step applied to a formula in a particular closure of β; therefore, that closure in β also succeeds.

(1, $\leftarrow$) Say $\beta \equiv \beta_1; C; \beta_2$, and C succeeds. Then we can get a successful computation of β by taking the successful computation of C and appending β_1 and β_2 on either side of each step.

(2) As in the proof for (1). □

We mention the number of steps in this lemma, and at various points from hereon in, because of the requirements of later proofs by induction. They are not really essential for a high-level understanding of the theorems.

Theorem 3.5 (SOS-Success Completeness of SOS/sa) If $(\theta : \alpha)$ has a successful SOS-computation, then it has a successful sequential-and computation of smaller or equal length.

Proof : By induction on the length of the SOS-computation. If the length is 0, then the computation is clearly sequential-and. Otherwise, let the length be n. If the first step applies to a formula on the top of the goal stack, then the result follows immediately from the induction hypothesis.

Otherwise, the first step is not on a formula on the top of the goal stack. We have two subcases:

- The first step is not on a disjunction; that is, the computation begins $(\theta : \mathbf{A}, \alpha) \stackrel{SOS}{\Rightarrow} (\theta' : \mathbf{A}, \alpha')$. By the induction hypothesis, the latter closure has a sequential-and computation of length $n-1$ or less. Again, we have two subcases.
  - $\mathbf{A}$ is not a disjunction. In this case, the sequential-and version of the tail of the computation begins $(\theta' : \mathbf{A}, \alpha') \stackrel{SOS}{\Rightarrow} (\theta'' : \alpha'', \alpha')$. Then we can form a computation starting

    $$(\theta : \mathbf{A}, \alpha) \stackrel{SOS}{\Rightarrow} (\theta''' : \alpha'', \alpha) \stackrel{SOS}{\Rightarrow} (\theta'' : \alpha'', \alpha')$$

    and ending with the sequential-and computation from before. (Here, we use reasoning similar to that in the Church-Rosser property proof.) By a second application of the induction hypothesis, the tail of this computation (length $n-1$) has a sequential-and computation; so the original closure has a sequential-and computation.
  - $\mathbf{A} \equiv \mathbf{B} \vee \mathbf{C}$. The sequential-and version of the tail of the computation begins $(\theta' : \mathbf{B} \vee \mathbf{C}, \alpha') \stackrel{SOS}{\Rightarrow} (\theta : \mathbf{B}, \alpha'); (\theta : \mathbf{C}, \alpha')$. By Lemma 3.4, one of these closures succeeds with a sequential-and computation of length n-2 or less; and we can proceed as in the proof of the last subcase.

- The first step is on some disjunction $\mathbf{B} \vee \mathbf{C}$; that is, the computation starts

$$(\theta : \alpha_1, \mathbf{B} \vee \mathbf{C}, \alpha_2) \stackrel{SOS}{\Rightarrow} (\theta : \alpha_1, \mathbf{B}, \alpha_2); (\theta : \alpha_1, \mathbf{C}, \alpha_2)$$

One of these closures (by Lemma 3.4) succeeds after at most $n-1$ steps. From this point, we can proceed as in the proof of the last subcase; that is, we can take the sequential-and version of the tail of this computation, interchange the first step of it with the disjunction step, and take the sequential-and version of this new tail.

□

Corollary 3.6 If β has a successful SOS-computation, then it has a successful sequential-and computation.

Proof : One closure in β must have a successful SOS-computation, so by the theorem, that closure must have a successful sequential-and computation. We can construct the sequential-and computation for β by appending the extraneous closures to either side of each step. □

The analogous relationship between sequential-or and sequential-both computations would be:

> If $(\theta : \alpha)$ has a successful sequential-or computation, then it has a successful sequential-both computation.

However, this result does not hold; consider the counterexample $(Loop()\&false) \vee true$. This has a successful sequential-or computation, because the first disjunct fails due to parallel processing of $false$; but it has no successful sequential-both computation.

4. Compositional Operational Semantics

Here I address the problem of non-compositionality discussed earlier. There are operational semantics which have greater compositionality, and at least one with a high degree of compositionality. These operational semantics are in the form of "single-step" systems, in which the relation between initial state and final state ("solution state") is determined by a formal system, rather than being the transitive closure of a set of rewriting rules. (See Plotkin [58] for more details about these styles of operational semantics.)

This style of operational semantics elucidates some of the higher-level properties of the basic SOS semantics, and will be used to some extent for proving, in the next chapters, the equivalences with the logical characterisations.

4.1. One-Stack Operational Semantics OS: Parallel Or

In the "one-stack" style of operational semantics OS, the relation $\stackrel{OS}{\Rightarrow}$ is no longer between two backtrack stacks, but rather between a closure and either a substitution or the element **fail**. OS thus "abstracts out" some of the irrelevant details of SOS concerning backtrack stacks, and concentrates on the relationship between a closure and one of its solutions.

In the next section, we will see a very similar operational semantics, OSso, which describes a parallel-and, sequential-or system. OS describes a parallel-and, parallel-or

Success rules.

=,1: $$\frac{}{(\theta : \mathbf{s} = \mathbf{t}) \overset{\text{OS}}{\Rightarrow} \theta\theta'} \quad (*a)$$

=,2: $$\frac{(\theta\theta' : \alpha_1, \alpha_2) \overset{\text{OS}}{\Rightarrow} \rho}{(\theta : \alpha_1, \mathbf{s} = \mathbf{t}, \alpha_2) \overset{\text{OS}}{\Rightarrow} \rho} \quad (*a)$$

&: $$\frac{(\theta : \alpha_1, \mathbf{B}, \mathbf{C}, \alpha_2) \overset{\text{OS}}{\Rightarrow} \rho}{(\theta : \alpha_1, \mathbf{B}\&\mathbf{C}, \alpha_2) \overset{\text{OS}}{\Rightarrow} \rho}$$

∨,1: $$\frac{(\theta : \alpha_1, \mathbf{B}, \alpha_2) \overset{\text{OS}}{\Rightarrow} \rho}{(\theta : \alpha_1, \mathbf{B} \vee \mathbf{C}, \alpha_2) \overset{\text{OS}}{\Rightarrow} \rho}$$

∨,2: $$\frac{(\theta : \alpha_1, \mathbf{C}, \alpha_2) \overset{\text{OS}}{\Rightarrow} \rho}{(\theta : \alpha_1, \mathbf{B} \vee \mathbf{C}, \alpha_2) \overset{\text{OS}}{\Rightarrow} \rho}$$

∃: $$\frac{(\theta : \alpha_1, \mathbf{B}[\mathbf{x} := \mathbf{x}'], \alpha_2) \overset{\text{OS}}{\Rightarrow} \rho}{(\theta : \alpha_1, \exists\mathbf{x}\ \mathbf{B}, \alpha_2) \overset{\text{OS}}{\Rightarrow} \rho} \quad (*b)$$

P: $$\frac{(\theta : \alpha_1, \mathbf{A}(\mathbf{t}_1, \ldots, \mathbf{t}_n), \alpha_2) \overset{\text{OS}}{\Rightarrow} \rho}{(\theta : \alpha_1, \mathbf{P}(\mathbf{t}_1, \ldots, \mathbf{t}_n), \alpha_2) \overset{\text{OS}}{\Rightarrow} \rho} \quad (*c)$$

Failure rules.

=,1: $$\frac{(\theta\theta' : \alpha_1, \alpha_2) \overset{\text{OS}}{\Rightarrow} \mathbf{fail}}{(\theta : \alpha_1, \mathbf{s} = \mathbf{t}, \alpha_2) \overset{\text{OS}}{\Rightarrow} \mathbf{fail}} \quad (*a)$$

=,2: $$\frac{}{(\theta : \alpha_1, \mathbf{s} = \mathbf{t}, \alpha_2) \overset{\text{OS}}{\Rightarrow} \mathbf{fail}} \quad (*d)$$

&: $$\frac{(\theta : \alpha_1, \mathbf{B}, \mathbf{C}, \alpha_2) \overset{\text{OS}}{\Rightarrow} \mathbf{fail}}{(\theta : \alpha_1, \mathbf{B}\&\mathbf{C}, \alpha_2) \overset{\text{OS}}{\Rightarrow} \mathbf{fail}}$$

∨: $$\frac{(\theta : \alpha_1, \mathbf{B}, \alpha_2) \overset{\text{OS}}{\Rightarrow} \mathbf{fail} \quad (\theta : \alpha_1, \mathbf{C}, \alpha_2) \overset{\text{OS}}{\Rightarrow} \mathbf{fail}}{(\theta : \alpha_1, \mathbf{B} \vee \mathbf{C}, \alpha_2) \overset{\text{OS}}{\Rightarrow} \mathbf{fail}}$$

∃: $$\frac{(\theta : \alpha_1, \mathbf{B}[\mathbf{x} := \mathbf{x}'], \alpha_2) \overset{\text{OS}}{\Rightarrow} \mathbf{fail}}{(\theta : \alpha_1, \exists\mathbf{x}\ \mathbf{B}, \alpha_2) \overset{\text{OS}}{\Rightarrow} \mathbf{fail}} \quad (*b)$$

P: $$\frac{(\theta : \alpha_1, \mathbf{A}(\mathbf{t}_1, \ldots, \mathbf{t}_n), \alpha_2) \overset{\text{OS}}{\Rightarrow} \mathbf{fail}}{(\theta : \alpha_1, \mathbf{P}(\mathbf{t}_1, \ldots, \mathbf{t}_n), \alpha_2) \overset{\text{OS}}{\Rightarrow} \mathbf{fail}} \quad (*c)$$

Side-conditions:

$(*a)$ θ' is the mgu of $\mathbf{s}\theta$ and $\mathbf{t}\theta$

$(*b)$ $\mathbf{x}'$ is a variable not appearing in the conclusion

$(*c)$ The definition $\mathbf{P}(\mathbf{x}_1, \ldots, \mathbf{x}_n) \leftrightarrow \mathbf{A}(\mathbf{x}_1, \ldots, \mathbf{x}_n)$ appears in the program Π

$(*d)$ $\mathbf{s}\theta$ and $\mathbf{t}\theta$ do not unify

Figure 2.3. Rules for the operational semantics OS.

system. The rules for OS are in Figure 2.3. The rules define a relation $\stackrel{OS}{\Rightarrow}$ between a closure and either a substitution ρ or the expression **fail**. The production relation thus "jumps" from initial to final state in a single step; it is in the natural-deduction-style rules for the parts of the formulae that the computation takes place.

Theorem 4.1 β has a successful computation in SOS iff some closure in it has a successful computation in OS.

Proof: ($\rightarrow$) By Lemma 3.4, some closure in β has a successful computation in SOS; we can do induction on the length of this SOS-computation. Each case follows fairly directly from the induction hypothesis. The only case that needs some care is the Unification, Failure case; there, we note that the failing closure cannot contribute to the success of β, so it must be one of the other closures which succeeds.

($\leftarrow$) We can build an SOS-computation from the OS-computation by reading out closures from bottom to top, sometimes adding the extraneous branches of disjunctions to the closure. □

Theorem 4.2 β has a failing computation in SOS iff all of its closures have failing computations in OS.

Proof : ($\rightarrow$) By induction on the length of the SOS-computation. Each case follows directly from the induction hypothesis.

($\leftarrow$) By induction on the total number of steps in all the OS-computations; the cases are on the lowest step in the OS-computation of the first closure in β. Each case follows directly from the induction hypothesis. □

We can form a sequential-and variant of OS, called OS/sa, by restricting α_1 in all rules to be the empty goal stack. This variant has the same completeness properties with respect to SOS/sa as OS has to SOS; we can see this by noting that the SOS computations which the above theorems construct from OS/sa computations are sequential-and, and similarly in the other direction.

4.2. One-Stack Operational Semantics OSso: Sequential Or

There is also a sequential-or variant of the above operational semantics, called OSso. (I write its name this way to indicate that it actually has different rules; I retain the slash notation for restricted variants of other operational semantics, such as SOS/so.) It is identical to OS, except that the $\vee, 2$ rule is replaced by the following rule:

$$\vee, 2\text{:}\ \frac{(\theta : \alpha_1, \mathbf{B}, \alpha_2) \stackrel{OS}{\Rightarrow} \mathbf{fail} \quad (\theta : \alpha_1, \mathbf{C}, \alpha_2) \stackrel{OS}{\Rightarrow} \rho}{(\theta : \alpha_1, \mathbf{B} \vee \mathbf{C}, \alpha_2) \stackrel{OS}{\Rightarrow} \rho}$$

The same kind of relationship exists between OSso and SOS/so as between OS and SOS. The failure-completeness theorem is exactly the same as with OS and SOS:

Theorem 4.3 β has a failing computation in SOS/so iff all of its closures have failing computations in OSso.

Proof : As above. □

The success-completeness theorem has a different form, but is proven in essentially the same way. It depends on the failure-completeness theorem.

Theorem 4.4 The backtrack stack $C_1; C_2; \ldots; C_n$ has a successful computation in SOS/so iff there is some i, $1 \leq i \leq n$, such that C_j has a failing computation in OSso for all $1 \leq j < i$, and C_i has a successful computation in OSso.

Proof : As above, except that in the case of a successful "or" computation we note that the SOS/so computation can and must fail on the left-hand branch before succeeding on the right-hand branch. □

There is a sequential-and variant of OSso as well, OSso/sa, in which α_1 must be empty for all rules. OSso/sa is sound and complete with respect to SP. Again, we can prove this by noting that the constructions that the above theorems make give SP computations from OSso/sa computations, and vice versa.

4.3. One-Formula Operational Semantics Csa

There is a very compositional equivalent of OS/sa, called Csa, in which the relation $\stackrel{\text{Csa}}{\Rightarrow}$ is not a binary relation between a closure and a substitution, but a ternary relation between an initial substitution, a single formula, and either a solution substitution or **fail**. Some of these rules have been presented before in a slightly different form [5] as the operational semantics called LP.

The rules for Csa are in Figure 2.4. The equivalence theorems between SOS/sa and Csa are as follows.

Theorem 4.5 $(\theta : \mathbf{A}_1, \ldots, \mathbf{A}_n) \stackrel{\text{OS/sa}}{\Rightarrow} \rho$ iff there are substitutions $\theta_1, \ldots, \theta_{n-1}$ such that $(\theta : \mathbf{A}_1 \stackrel{\text{Csa}}{\Rightarrow} \theta_1), (\theta_1 : \mathbf{A}_2 \stackrel{\text{Csa}}{\Rightarrow} \theta_2), \ldots (\theta_{n-2} : \mathbf{A}_{n-1} \stackrel{\text{Csa}}{\Rightarrow} \theta_{n-1}), (\theta_{n-1} : \mathbf{A}_n \stackrel{\text{Csa}}{\Rightarrow} \rho)$.

Proof : ($\rightarrow$) By induction on the size of the OS/sa-computation. Cases are on the bottommost rule application.

=, 1 and 2: The first step finds the most general unifier θ'. The result follows immediately from the induction hypothesis.

&: Let $\mathbf{A}_1 \equiv \mathbf{B}\&\mathbf{C}$. By the induction hypothesis, we have that $\theta : \mathbf{B} \stackrel{\text{Csa}}{\Rightarrow} \theta'$ and $\theta' : \mathbf{C} \stackrel{\text{Csa}}{\Rightarrow} \theta_1$; the result follows immediately.

$\vee$ (1 and 2), $\exists$, **P**: the result follows directly from the induction hypothesis.

($\leftarrow$) By induction on the structure of the Csa-computations. Cases are on the form of $\mathbf{A}_1$, and are straightforward. □

The more significant corollary says that the set of successful *queries* is the same for the two operational semantics.

Corollary 4.6 The query **A** succeeds in SOS/sa iff it succeeds in Csa.

Proof : By the equivalence of OS/sa to SOS/sa, $(() : \mathbf{A})$ succeeds in SOS/sa iff is succeeds in OS/sa; and this happens, by the theorem, iff it succeeds in Csa. □

We have the corresponding results for failure.

Success:

=: $$\frac{}{\theta : \mathbf{s} = \mathbf{t} \overset{\mathrm{Csa}}{\Rightarrow} \theta\theta'} \quad (*a)$$

&: $$\frac{\theta : \mathbf{B} \overset{\mathrm{Csa}}{\Rightarrow} \theta' \quad \theta' : \mathbf{C} \overset{\mathrm{Csa}}{\Rightarrow} \rho}{\theta : \mathbf{B}\&\mathbf{C} \overset{\mathrm{Csa}}{\Rightarrow} \rho}$$

∨, 1: $$\frac{\theta : \mathbf{B} \overset{\mathrm{Csa}}{\Rightarrow} \rho}{\theta : \mathbf{B} \vee \mathbf{C} \overset{\mathrm{Csa}}{\Rightarrow} \rho}$$

∨, 2: $$\frac{\theta : \mathbf{C} \overset{\mathrm{Csa}}{\Rightarrow} \rho}{\theta : \mathbf{B} \vee \mathbf{C} \overset{\mathrm{Csa}}{\Rightarrow} \rho}$$

∃: $$\frac{\theta : \mathbf{B}[\mathbf{x} := \mathbf{x}'] \overset{\mathrm{Csa}}{\Rightarrow} \rho}{\theta : \exists \mathbf{x}\ \mathbf{B} \overset{\mathrm{Csa}}{\Rightarrow} \rho} \quad (*b)$$

P: $$\frac{\theta : \mathbf{A}(\mathbf{t}_1, \ldots, \mathbf{t}_n) \overset{\mathrm{Csa}}{\Rightarrow} \rho}{\theta : \mathbf{P}(\mathbf{t}_1, \ldots, \mathbf{t}_n) \overset{\mathrm{Csa}}{\Rightarrow} \rho} \quad (*c)$$

Failure:

=: $$\frac{}{\theta : \mathbf{s} = \mathbf{t} \overset{\mathrm{Csa}}{\Rightarrow} \mathbf{fail}} \quad (*d)$$

&, 1: $$\frac{\theta : \mathbf{B} \overset{\mathrm{Csa}}{\Rightarrow} \mathbf{fail}}{\theta : \mathbf{B}\&\mathbf{C} \overset{\mathrm{Csa}}{\Rightarrow} \mathbf{fail}}$$

&, 2: $$\frac{\theta : \mathbf{B} \overset{\mathrm{Csa}}{\Rightarrow} \theta' \quad \theta' : \mathbf{C} \overset{\mathrm{Csa}}{\Rightarrow} \mathbf{fail}}{\theta : \mathbf{B}\&\mathbf{C} \overset{\mathrm{Csa}}{\Rightarrow} \mathbf{fail}}$$

∨: $$\frac{\theta : \mathbf{B} \overset{\mathrm{Csa}}{\Rightarrow} \mathbf{fail} \quad \theta : \mathbf{C} \overset{\mathrm{Csa}}{\Rightarrow} \mathbf{fail}}{\theta : \mathbf{B} \vee \mathbf{C} \overset{\mathrm{Csa}}{\Rightarrow} \mathbf{fail}}$$

∃: $$\frac{\theta : \mathbf{B}[\mathbf{x} := \mathbf{x}'] \overset{\mathrm{Csa}}{\Rightarrow} \mathbf{fail}}{\theta : \exists \mathbf{x}\ \mathbf{B} \overset{\mathrm{Csa}}{\Rightarrow} \mathbf{fail}} \quad (*b)$$

P: $$\frac{\theta : \mathbf{A}(\mathbf{t}_1, \ldots, \mathbf{t}_n) \overset{\mathrm{Csa}}{\Rightarrow} \mathbf{fail}}{\theta : \mathbf{P}(\mathbf{t}_1, \ldots, \mathbf{t}_n) \overset{\mathrm{Csa}}{\Rightarrow} \mathbf{fail}} \quad (*c)$$

Side-conditions:

$(*a)$ θ' is the mgu of $\mathbf{s}\theta$ and $\mathbf{t}\theta$

$(*b)$ $\mathbf{x}'$ is a variable not appearing in the conclusion

$(*c)$ The definition $\mathbf{P}(\mathbf{x}_1, \ldots, \mathbf{x}_n) \leftrightarrow \mathbf{A}(\mathbf{x}_1, \ldots, \mathbf{x}_n)$ appears in the program Π

$(*d)$ $\mathbf{s}\theta$ and $\mathbf{t}\theta$ do not unify

Figure 2.4. Rules for the Operational Semantics Csa.

Theorem 4.7 $(\theta_0 : \mathbf{A}_1, \mathbf{A}_2, \ldots, \mathbf{A}_n) \stackrel{\text{SOS/sa}}{\Rightarrow}$ **fail** iff for some i, $1 \leq i \leq n$, we have that $(\theta_0 : \mathbf{A}_1 \stackrel{\text{Csa}}{\Rightarrow} \theta_1), (\theta_1 : \mathbf{A}_2 \stackrel{\text{Csa}}{\Rightarrow} \theta_2), \ldots, (\theta_{i-2} : \mathbf{A}_{i-1} \stackrel{\text{Csa}}{\Rightarrow} \theta_{i-1}), (\theta_{i-1} : \mathbf{A}_i \stackrel{\text{Csa}}{\Rightarrow}$ **fail**).

Proof : $(\rightarrow)$ By induction on the bottommost rule application.

=, 1: by the induction hypothesis.

=, 2: immediate.

&: By the induction hypothesis, either $\theta_0 : \mathbf{B} \stackrel{\text{Csa}}{\Rightarrow}$ **fail** (in which case **B&C** also fails); or $\theta_0 : \mathbf{B} \stackrel{\text{Csa}}{\Rightarrow} \theta'$ and $\theta' : \mathbf{C} \stackrel{\text{Csa}}{\Rightarrow}$ **fail** (in which case **B&C** also fails); or $\theta_0 : \mathbf{B} \stackrel{\text{Csa}}{\Rightarrow} \theta'$ and $\theta' : \mathbf{C} \stackrel{\text{Csa}}{\Rightarrow} \theta_2$ (in which case $\theta_0 :$ **B&C** $\stackrel{\text{Csa}}{\Rightarrow} \theta_1$), but one of the later $\mathbf{A}_i$'s fails, and the result follows from the induction hypothesis.

$\vee$, $\exists$, **P**: by the induction hypothesis.

$(\leftarrow)$ By induction on the structure of the Csa-computations. Cases are on the form of $\mathbf{A}_1$, and are straightforward. □

Corollary 4.8 The query **A** fails in SOS/sa iff it fails in Csa.

Proof : By the equivalence of OS/sa to SOS/sa, and by the theorem. □

In summary, OS and its sequential-and variant OS/sa, OSso and its sequential-and variant OSso/sa, and Csa shed some light on the structure of computations in SOS and its variants by making computations more compositional. However, SOS remains the only operational semantics we have found so far in which all four control disciplines are simple restricted variants of the main system.

SOS is also the simplest system, having only six rules; it seems that the various properties of success and failure brought out by the compositional operational semantics require more rules. Later, we will be proving the soundness and completeness of various proof-theoretic characterisations with respect to the operational semantics; to do this, we will sometimes use SOS because of the lower number of rules, and sometimes use one of the other operational semantics for their compositionality.

Finally, I should note that in all the equivalence theorems given in this section, whenever a computation in one system is constructed from several in another (or vice versa), the total number of rule applications is preserved in the other system. I did not include this information in the statements of the theorems or proofs because it would have cluttered them up unnecessarily; but readers should be able to see this by inspection of the proofs. We will need this property occasionally when we do inductions on the lengths of computations.

5. Some Properties of Existential Quantification

In the soundness and completeness proofs in later chapters, we will need some results about the behaviour of existential quantifiers. These, in turn, depend on more general results about the behaviour of backtrack stacks under subsitutitions. I group these results together in this section because they are essentially inductive proofs in the operational semantics.

5.1. Failure

Some properties of failure are shared by all variants of the operational semantics. One such property is that if a computation fails, it also fails under any more specific substitution.

Lemma 5.1 If $(\theta : \alpha)$ fails in SOS, then for all substitutions ρ, $(\theta\rho : \alpha)$ fails in SOS with a smaller or equal number of steps; and if the original computation was sequential-and (and/or sequential-or), so is the new computation.

Proof : By induction on the number of steps in the SOS computation, constructing a computation for $(\theta\rho : \alpha)$ from that for $(\theta : \alpha)$. Cases are on the form of the first rule.

&, Defined Predicate: Follows immediately from the induction hypothesis.

$\vee$: Both of the resultant closures must fail, with shorter computations than the original. Thus, by the induction hypothesis, the original closure fails.

$\exists$: We can choose $\mathbf{x}'$ in the rule so that it does not appear in ρ either.

Unification, success: One of the α formulae is $\mathbf{s} = \mathbf{t}$, and $\mathbf{s}\theta$ and $\mathbf{t}\theta$ unify. Let their unifier be θ'. Now consider $\mathbf{s}\theta\rho$ and $\mathbf{t}\theta\rho$. Either they do not unify (in which case we have the result) or they have an mgu θ''. But by the properties of mgu, since θ' is the mgu of $\mathbf{s}\theta$ and $\mathbf{t}\theta$, there must be a ρ' such that $\theta'\rho' \equiv \rho\theta''$. Thus, by the induction hypothesis (taking ρ to be ρ'), the result holds.

Unification, failure: One of the α formulae is $\mathbf{s} = \mathbf{t}$. Since $\mathbf{s}\theta$ and $\mathbf{t}\theta$ do not unify (there is no substitution that makes them identical), they cannot unify under any more specific substitution. □

This lemma is required for an important theorem, which talks specifically about existential quantification.

Theorem 5.2 ("Fails-all-fail") If $(\theta : \exists \mathbf{x}\ \mathbf{A})$ fails in SOS (or some variant thereof), then for all $\mathbf{t}$, $(\theta : \mathbf{A}[\mathbf{x} := \mathbf{t}])$ fails in SOS (or the variant) with a smaller number of steps.

Proof : The computation of $(\theta : \exists \mathbf{x}\ \mathbf{A})$ must start by making one step to $(\theta : \mathbf{A}[\mathbf{x} := \mathbf{x}'])$. By the lemma above, $(\theta[\mathbf{x}' := \mathbf{t}] : \mathbf{A}[\mathbf{x} := \mathbf{x}'])$ must fail. But this closure behaves identically to $(\theta : \mathbf{A}[\mathbf{x} := \mathbf{t}])$, in either SOS or SOS/sa. □

So if the existential closure of a query fails, then every closed instance of it fails. But the converse is not true: it is not the case, in any variant of the operational semantics, that if all closed instances fail, then the existential closure fails. The paradigmatic counterexample here is the following. Consider the definition of the predicate "Inflist", which "succeeds" iff its argument is an infinite list:

$$Inflist(x) \leftrightarrow \exists xh \exists xt(x = [xh|xt] \& Inflist(xt))$$

This predicate clearly never does succeed, since we are still working in the domain of first order terms. However, whereas every closed instance of the query $Inflist(y)$ fails, the query $\exists y(Inflist(y))$ paradoxically diverges, looking for an infinite list but finding only ever-longer incomplete finite lists.

5.2. Success

A complementary set of results to the ones in the previous section are ones which deal with success: if a query succeeds, then it succeeds with all more specific substitutions that are still more general than the solution substitution.

Definition 5.3 We say that θ' is *more specific than* θ, or that θ is *more general than* θ', if there is a ρ such that $\theta' \equiv \theta\rho$.

Lemma 5.4 If $(\theta : \alpha)$ succeeds in SOS with the solution θ_f, then, for any θ' more specific than θ but more general than θ_f, $(\theta' : \alpha)$ succeeds in SOS with the solution θ_f with a smaller or equal number of steps. Moreover, if the original computation was sequential-and (and/or sequential-or), so is the new computation.

Proof : By induction on the number of steps in the SOS-computation. Cases are on the first step.

&, Defined Predicates: Follows directly from the induction hypothesis.

$\vee$: If the original computation was parallel-or, then one of the resultant closures must succeed (by Lemma 3.4), so the result follows by the induction hypothesis. If the original computation was sequential-or, then either the first closure succeeds (in which case the result follows by the induction hyporthesis), or else the first closure fails (in which case, by the fails-all-fail lemma, it fails under any more specific substitution) and the second succeeds (so the result follows from the induction hypothesis).

$\exists$: We can choose $\mathbf{x}'$ so that is does not appear in θ' either; then the result follows from the induction hypothesis.

Unification, success: Let $\theta' \equiv \theta\rho$. One of the α formulae is of the form $\mathbf{s} = \mathbf{t}$, and $\mathbf{s}\theta$ and $\mathbf{t}\theta$ have an mgu, ρ'. We can prove by a simple induction that $\mathbf{s}\theta_f \equiv \mathbf{t}\theta_f$, and θ_f is more specific than θ'; so $\mathbf{s}$ and $\mathbf{t}$ unify under θ' too; let their mgu be θ''. Thus, $\mathbf{s}\theta\rho\theta'' \equiv \mathbf{t}\theta\rho\theta''$; by the properties of mgu (ρ'), there must be a ρ'' such that $\rho'\rho'' \equiv \rho\theta''$. By the induction hypothesis (on ρ''), we have the result.

Note that there is no case for failure of unification, as we have assumed that the closure succeeds. □

Theorem 5.5 ("Succeeds-one-succeeds") If $(\theta : \exists \mathbf{x}\ \mathbf{B})$ succeeds in SOS (or some variant thereof) with solution θ_f, then there is a closed $\mathbf{t}$ such that $(\theta : \mathbf{B}[\mathbf{x} := \mathbf{t}])$ succeeds in SOS (or the variant) with a smaller number of steps.

Proof : Let the first step in the computation replace $\mathbf{x}$ by $\mathbf{x}'$, and let $\mathbf{t}$ be any closed instance of $x'\theta_f$. By a simple induction we can prove that $(\theta : \exists \mathbf{x}\ (\mathbf{B}\&\mathbf{x} = \mathbf{t}))$ succeeds with solution $\theta_f[\mathbf{x}' := \mathbf{t}]$. But then by the lemma, $(\theta[\mathbf{x}' := \mathbf{t}] : \exists \mathbf{x}\ (\mathbf{B}\&\mathbf{x} = \mathbf{t}))$ succeeds, after making two steps to $(\theta[\mathbf{x}' := \mathbf{t}] : \mathbf{B}[\mathbf{x} := \mathbf{x}'], \mathbf{x}' := \mathbf{t})$; this closure will behave essentially identically to $(\theta : \mathbf{B}[\mathbf{x} := \mathbf{t}])$, which must therefore succeed. □

Thus, if the existential closure of a query succeeds, then there is some instance of it which succeeds.

5.3. Solution Completeness

The converse of the theorems in the last section is one which says that if a solution exists, the system will find one. This is true only in the case of parallel-or systems. It is a bit more convenient to prove this using OS rather than SOS.

Lemma 5.6 If θ' is more specific than θ, and $(\theta' : \alpha) \stackrel{OS}{\Rightarrow} \theta_f$, then there is a θ'_f such that $(\theta : \alpha) \stackrel{OS}{\Rightarrow} \theta'_f$. Moreover, if the original computation was sequential-and, then so is the new computation.

		Stack-of-Stacks	One-Stack	One-Formula
Par. "Or"	Par. "And"	SOS	OS	
	Seq. "And"	SOS/sa	OS/sa	Csa
Seq. "Or"	Par. "And"	SOS/so	OSso	
	Seq. "And"	SOS/soa ("SP")	OSso/sa	

Figure 2.5. Classification of operational semantics.

Proof: By induction on the number of rule applications in the OS-computation. Cases are on the bottommost rule applied.

Success, $=, 1$, Success, $=, 2$: One of the α formulae is $\mathbf{s} = \mathbf{t}$, and the mgu of $\mathbf{s}\theta'$ and $\mathbf{t}\theta'$ is some ρ. Thus we know that $\mathbf{s}\theta'\rho \equiv \mathbf{t}\theta'\rho$, so $\mathbf{s}\theta$ and $\mathbf{t}\theta$ unify, resulting in a substitution which is at least as specific as $\theta'\rho$. In the case of $=, 1$, the result follows immediately; in the case of $=, 2$, the result follows from the induction hypothesis.

Success, $\&; \vee, 1; \vee, 2; \exists; \mathbf{P}$: follows directly from the induction hypothesis. In the $\exists$ case, if the new variable does not appear in θ', then it does not appear in θ either. □

Theorem 5.7 ("One-succeeds-succeeds") If there is a $\mathbf{t}$ such that $(\theta : \mathbf{B}[\mathbf{x} := \mathbf{t}])$ succeeds in SOS (resp. SOS/sa), then $(\theta : \exists\mathbf{x}\ \mathbf{B})$ succeeds in SOS (resp. SOS/sa).

Proof: The first step of the computation of $(\theta : \exists\mathbf{x}\ \mathbf{B})$ is to $(\theta : \mathbf{B}[\mathbf{x} := \mathbf{x}'])$. But we know that $(\theta[\mathbf{x}' := \mathbf{t}] : \mathbf{B}[\mathbf{x} := \mathbf{x}'])$ succeeds; so by the lemma, and the equivalence of OS (OS/sa) to SOS (SOS/sa), $(\theta : \mathbf{B}[\mathbf{x} := \mathbf{x}'])$ succeeds as well. □

This theorem does not work in the sequential-or case, because there the rule $\vee, 2$ depends upon a failing computation of the left-hand disjunct, which may not exist. For instance, although the closure $(() : \mathit{Inflist}(3) \vee 3 = 3)$ succeeds in both OS and OSso, the closure $(() : \exists x(\mathit{Inflist}(x) \vee x = x))$ succeeds only in OS, and diverges in OSso.

Finally, a note about the statements of all the theorems in this section: wherever they mention one computation taking fewer steps than another, the result applies not only to the SOS variants mentioned, but also to any equivalent compositional operational semantics. This is because the number of rule applications in the compositional semantics computations is the same as the number of steps in the corresponding SOS variant.

6. Summary and Classification of Queries

I have given a number of different operational semantics here, but they fall into four basic categories: namely, the four different combinations of parallel or sequential "and" and parallel or sequential "or". The OS variants and Csa fall into one category or another depending on their equivalence properties with respect to the SOS variants. Figure 2.5 summarises this classification.

Queries themselves can be classified by how they behave in the various control disciplines. Figure 2.6 summarises this information. There are two classes of failing queries: one class all of whose queries fail in all control disciplines, and a wider one whose queries fail in all parallel-and control disciplines. There are three classes of successful queries: one all of whose queries succeed in all disciplines, a wider one all of whose queries succeed in all disciplines except SP, and a still wider one all of whose queries succeed in all parallel-or disciplines.

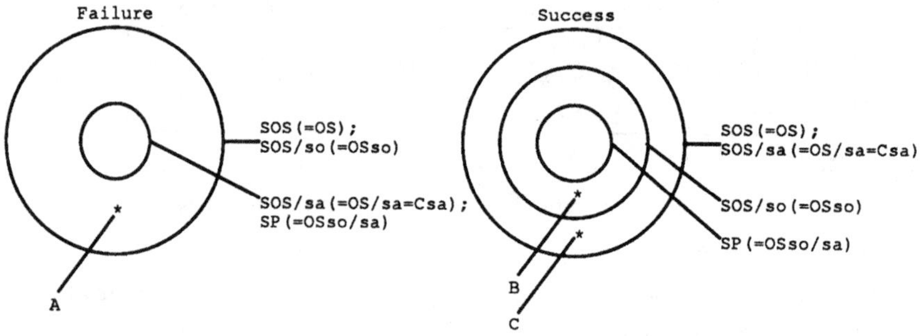

Figure 2.6. Classification of queries as to their behaviour in the variants of SOS. **A**, **B**, and **C** are example formulae within these classes; $\mathbf{A} \equiv \mathit{Loop}()\&\mathit{false}$; $\mathbf{B} \equiv (\mathit{Loop}()\&\mathit{false}) \vee \mathit{true}$; $\mathbf{C} \equiv \mathit{Loop}() \vee \mathit{true}$.

Chapter 3

Characterising Parallel Systems

In this chapter, I present a sequent calculus which characterises the outer two circles of the Venn diagram in Figure 2.6. In this calculus, we can state and prove assertions about the success and failure of queries in parallel logic programming systems. Assertions can be *signed formulae*, which are essentially expressions of the form $S(\mathbf{A})$ ("**A** succeeds") or $F(\mathbf{A})$ ("**A** fails"); assertions can also be expressions built up from signed formulae with the usual connectives of first order logic.

The sequent calculus is in two distinct parts. LKE is a very typical classical sequent calculus with equality, and deals with connectives at the top level of assertions. PAR is a set of simple axioms which describe how the goal-formula connectives distribute over the signs S and F; for instance, $S(\mathbf{B}\&\mathbf{C}) \leftrightarrow S(\mathbf{B})\&S(\mathbf{C})$. LKE will also be used in the next chapter, where we shall deal with sequential systems; but there, PAR will be replaced by a set of analogous axioms, SEQ.

Associated with assertions and sequents is a notion of validity. For reasons which will be discussed in Chapter 5, we cannot have a finitary sequent calculus which is both sound (all derivable sequents are valid) and complete (all valid sequents are derivable); however, the calculus in this chapter is sound, and has various useful completeness properties weaker than full completeness.

This sequent calculus can therefore be seen as a semantic characterisation of parallel Prolog; or, conversely, as a logic with respect to which parallel Prolog enjoys soundness and completeness properties. It can also be used to prove properties of programs. These issues will be discussed in greater detail in the final section of this chapter.

1. Overview and Definitions

I should first give a detailed overview of what we are trying to accomplish and how.

Our main concern is that of characterising, via proof systems, the success or failure of queries to the parallel logic programming system SOS. We could do this by trying to characterise the sequence of satisfying substitutions from a goal formula, but this inevitably seems to lead us back to the realm of operational semantics. If we instead stick to just characterising *whether* the query succeeds or fails, we can express the behaviour of a goal formula **A** by expressions of the form $S(\mathbf{A})$ or $F(\mathbf{A})$, to be read as "**A** succeeds" or "**A** fails", respectively. These expressions will be called *signed (goal) formulae.* (For technical reasons, as we will see, it will be necessary to distinguish the subclass of queries which fail without making predicate calls.)

Signed formulae could act as the judgments of our proof system, but we often will want to make more complex assertions about success or failure: "For all x there is a y such that $P(x,y)$ succeeds," or "For all l, if $List(l)$ succeeds then $\exists n\ Length(l,n)$ succeeds," for instance. We can therefore define *assertions* as a class of pseudo-formulae built up from signed formulae and equality formulae by the classical connectives. In assertions, as we will see, the S and F signs act much like modalities; but we cannot define the syntax of assertions as we would define formulae in modal logic, because only goal formulae can appear within a sign.

Finally, we need to decide what style of proof system to use: natural deduction, sequent calculus, tableaux, or some other style. I have chosen to use the sequent calculus style because it seems to provide more uniformity and expressive power than the natural deduction style, and because its organisation of rules is more natural for our purposes than the tableau style.

We therefore have the following definitions.

Definition 1.1 A *signed formula* is an expression of one of the forms $S(\mathbf{A})$, $F^Y(\mathbf{A})$, or $F^N(\mathbf{A})$, where $\mathbf{A}$ is a goal formula. The informal meaning of these expressions is intended to be, respectively, "$\mathbf{A}$ succeeds", "$\mathbf{A}$ fails, possibly performing predicate calls", and "$\mathbf{A}$ fails without performing predicate calls". We will sometimes use the notation $F(\mathbf{A})$ to mean either $F^Y(\mathbf{A})$ or $F^N(\mathbf{A})$, when either it does not matter which we mean or it is temporarily being used to mean consistently one thing. Similarly, we use the notation $\sigma(\mathbf{A})$ to mean either $S(\mathbf{A})$, $F^Y(\mathbf{A})$, or $F^N(\mathbf{A})$.

An *assertion* is an expression of the following BNF syntax:

$$\mathbf{A} ::= \mathbf{A}_1 \& \mathbf{A}_2 \mid \neg\mathbf{A} \mid \exists \mathbf{x}\mathbf{A} \mid \mathbf{s} = \mathbf{t} \mid \sigma(\mathbf{G})$$

where $\mathbf{G}$ is a goal formula. We will generally use $\mathbf{A}$, $\mathbf{B}$, $\mathbf{C}$, $\mathbf{D}$ as metavariables ranging over assertions as well as goal formulae; their use will be unambiguous.

We will define $\mathbf{B} \vee \mathbf{C}$ as $\neg(\neg\mathbf{B}\&\neg\mathbf{C})$, $\mathbf{B} \supset \mathbf{C}$ as $\neg(\mathbf{B}\&\neg\mathbf{C})$, and $\forall\mathbf{x}\ \mathbf{B}$ as $\neg(\exists\mathbf{x}\ \neg\mathbf{B})$.

Notions of *free and bound variables* for signed formulae and assertions will be a straightforward extension of those for formulae.

A *sequent* is an expression of the form

$$\mathbf{A}_1, \ldots, \mathbf{A}_n \rightarrow \mathbf{D}_1, \ldots, \mathbf{D}_m$$

where $n, m \geq 0$ and each of the $\mathbf{A}_i$'s and $\mathbf{D}_j$'s is an assertion. We will treat each side of the sequent as a finite *set* of assertions. Γ and Δ will range over sequences/sets of assertions: we will write Γ, Δ for the union of the two sets Γ and Δ; $\Gamma, \mathbf{A}$ for the union of Γ with $\{\mathbf{A}\}$; and so on.

We will generally refer to the sequence of formulae on the left-hand side of the arrow as the *antecedent*, and that on the right-hand side as the *consequent* of the sequent.

We now need to have a notion of *validity* which expresses our intended interpretation of the truth of assertions. In keeping with the approach of basing the logic on the operational semantics, I will give an inductive definition of validity of a closed assertion, at the base of which are simple notions of validity of closed equality formulae and closed signed goal formulae.

In this chapter, we will be concerned with validity with respect to the parallel operational semantics SOS. In the next chapter, the sequential operational semantics SP will concern us, but the definition of validity will be essentially the same, so I will express this notion in more general terms.

Definition 1.2 A closed assertion is *valid* with respect to a particular operational semantics O (chosen from the variants of SOS) and program Π just in the following cases.

- $\mathbf{B}\&\mathbf{C}$ is valid iff both $\mathbf{B}$ and $\mathbf{C}$ are valid.
- $\neg\mathbf{B}$ is valid iff $\mathbf{B}$ is not valid.
- $\exists\mathbf{x}\ \mathbf{B}$ is valid iff there is a closed term $\mathbf{t}$ such that $\mathbf{B}[\mathbf{x} := \mathbf{t}]$ is valid.
- $\mathbf{s} = \mathbf{t}$ is valid iff $\mathbf{s}$ and $\mathbf{t}$ are identical.
- $S(\mathbf{A})$ is valid iff the backtrack stack $(() : \mathbf{A})$ succeeds in the operational semantics O.
- $F^Y(\mathbf{A})$ is valid iff the backtrack stack $(() : \mathbf{A})$ fails in the operational semantics O.
- $F^N(\mathbf{A})$ is valid iff the backtrack stack $(() : \mathbf{A})$ can fail in the operational semantics O without performing any Defined Predicate steps.

Note that the negation sign has nothing to do with negation as failure in this context; $\neg S(A)$ means that $\mathbf{A}$ does not succeed, which might mean either that it fails or that it diverges.

We will also speak of the validity of a sequent, which is based on the validity of formulae and the notion of substitution.

Definition 1.3 A sequent $\mathbf{A}_1, \ldots, \mathbf{A}_n \rightarrow \mathbf{D}_1, \ldots, \mathbf{D}_m$ is valid iff for every θ which makes all the assertions in the sequent closed, either some $\mathbf{A}_i\theta$ is not valid or else some $\mathbf{D}_j\theta$ is valid.

It should be clear that the sequent $\mathbf{A}_1, \ldots, \mathbf{A}_n \rightarrow \mathbf{D}_1, \ldots, \mathbf{D}_m$ is valid iff the formula $\forall[\mathbf{A}_1\& \ldots \&\mathbf{A}_n \supset \mathbf{D}_1 \vee \ldots \vee \mathbf{D}_m]$ is valid, as in the usual presentations of the classical sequent calculus.

The notion of failure without performing Defined Predicate steps will recur frequently. For brevity, in this context I will use the expression "flat failure", and say that a query "fails flatly".

The effect of these definitions is to say that the sequent calculi which we will build will be *program logics*: logical systems in which properties of programs and queries can be stated and proved. Like Floyd-Hoare and other program logics [40], the syntactic elements of programs and queries will appear in the judgments of the proof systems, as sub-expressions of these judgments. Unlike traditional program logics for imperative and functional programming, however, the programming language being talked about will itself be logical.

In fact, since we have separate definitions for goal formulae and assertions, we could have chosen to use syntactically distinct connectives within goals (say $\hat{\&}, \hat{\vee}, \hat{\exists}$) to emphasise this separation of levels. The task of the program logic will be to clarify the correspondence between the connectives in queries and programs (the connectives within the signs) and those in assertions (the connectives outside the signs).

1. Equality, first group.

Eq: $$\frac{}{\Gamma \to \mathbf{t} = \mathbf{t}, \Delta}$$

Ineq: $$\frac{}{\Gamma, \mathbf{f}(\mathbf{s}_1, \ldots, \mathbf{s}_n) = \mathbf{g}(\mathbf{t}_1, \ldots, \mathbf{t}_m) \to \Delta} \qquad (*a)$$

Comp: $$\frac{\Gamma, \mathbf{s}_1 = \mathbf{t}_1, \ldots, \mathbf{s}_n = \mathbf{t}_n \to \Delta}{\Gamma, \mathbf{f}(\mathbf{s}_1, \ldots, \mathbf{s}_n) = \mathbf{f}(\mathbf{t}_1, \ldots, \mathbf{t}_n) \to \Delta}$$

2. Connectives.

&, l: $$\frac{\Gamma, \mathbf{B}, \mathbf{C} \to \Delta}{\Gamma, \mathbf{B}\&\mathbf{C} \to \Delta}$$ &, r: $$\frac{\Gamma \to \mathbf{B}, \Delta \quad \Gamma \to \mathbf{C}, \Delta}{\Gamma \to \mathbf{B}\&\mathbf{C}, \Delta}$$

∃, l: $$\frac{\Gamma, \mathbf{B}[\mathbf{x} := \mathbf{y}] \to \Delta}{\Gamma, \exists \mathbf{x}\ \mathbf{B} \to \Delta}$$ (*b) ∃, r: $$\frac{\Gamma \to \mathbf{B}[\mathbf{x} := \mathbf{t}], \Delta}{\Gamma \to \exists \mathbf{x}\ \mathbf{B}, \Delta}$$

¬, l: $$\frac{\Gamma \to \mathbf{B}, \Delta}{\Gamma, \neg \mathbf{B} \to \Delta}$$ ¬, r: $$\frac{\Gamma, \mathbf{B} \to \Delta}{\Gamma \to \neg \mathbf{B}, \Delta}$$

Side-conditions:
(*a) $\mathbf{f} \not\equiv \mathbf{g}$
(*b) $\mathbf{y}$ does not occur free in the lower sequent

Figure 3.1. Rules for proof system LKE, part I.

2. LKE and Its Soundness

The sequent calculus in this chapter will have two parts: a set of rules concerned only with assertions, which will also be used in the next chapter, and a set of axioms concerning signed formulae, which will be used only in this one. The first part is the subject of this section.

The assertion rules are collectively called LKE, because they are essentially Gentzen's LK ("Logischer Klassischer," or classical-logic) sequent calculus [36], augmented with Equality rules. Readers will recognise the similarity between these rules and those found in Gentzen's original description, given the common modern practice of considering each side of a sequent as a set.

The rules of LKE are in Figures 3.1 and 3.2, classified into groups. We will generally refer to the upper sequents in any application of a rule as the *premisses* of the rule, and the lower sequent as the *conclusion.* We will find it very useful to have rules for the defined connectives ∨, ⊃, and ∀, which are in Figure 3.3. These rules are easily derivable by expanding the connectives in question into their definitions.

We would like to prove the soundness of LKE alone, but actually we will want to

3. Equality, second group.

Occ: $\dfrac{}{\Gamma, \mathbf{s} = \mathbf{t} \rightarrow \Delta}$ $(*c)$

Sub, l: $\dfrac{\Gamma, \mathbf{s} = \mathbf{t}, \mathbf{A}(\mathbf{s}) \rightarrow \Delta}{\Gamma, \mathbf{s} = \mathbf{t}, \mathbf{A}(\mathbf{t}) \rightarrow \Delta}$ Sub, r: $\dfrac{\Gamma, \mathbf{s} = \mathbf{t} \rightarrow \mathbf{A}(\mathbf{s}), \Delta}{\Gamma, \mathbf{s} = \mathbf{t} \rightarrow \mathbf{A}(\mathbf{t}), \Delta}$

4. Structural rules.

Ax: $\dfrac{}{\Gamma, \mathbf{A} \rightarrow \mathbf{A}, \Delta}$ Cut: $\dfrac{\Gamma_1 \rightarrow \mathbf{A}, \Delta_1 \quad \Gamma_2, \mathbf{A} \rightarrow \Delta_2}{\Gamma_1, \Gamma_2 \rightarrow \Delta_1, \Delta_2}$

Thin, l: $\dfrac{\Gamma \rightarrow \Delta}{\Gamma, \mathbf{A} \rightarrow \Delta}$ Thin, r: $\dfrac{\Gamma \rightarrow \Delta}{\Gamma \rightarrow \mathbf{A}, \Delta}$

Side-conditions:
$(*c)$ **s** is a proper subterm of **t** or vice versa

Figure 3.2. Rules for proof system LKE, part II.

5. Derivable rules for defined connectives.

$\vee$, l: $\dfrac{\Gamma, \mathbf{B} \rightarrow \Delta \quad \Gamma, \mathbf{C} \rightarrow \Delta}{\Gamma, \mathbf{B} \vee \mathbf{C} \rightarrow \Delta}$ $\vee$, r: $\dfrac{\Gamma \rightarrow \mathbf{B}, \mathbf{C}, \Delta}{\Gamma \rightarrow \mathbf{B} \vee \mathbf{C}, \Delta}$

$\supset$, l: $\dfrac{\Gamma \rightarrow \mathbf{B}, \Delta \quad \Gamma, \mathbf{C} \rightarrow \Delta}{\Gamma, \mathbf{B} \supset \mathbf{C} \rightarrow \Delta}$ $\supset$, r: $\dfrac{\Gamma, \mathbf{B} \rightarrow \mathbf{C}, \Delta}{\Gamma \rightarrow \mathbf{B} \supset \mathbf{C}, \Delta}$

$\forall$, l: $\dfrac{\Gamma, \mathbf{B}[\mathbf{x} := \mathbf{t}] \rightarrow \Delta}{\Gamma, \forall \mathbf{x}\ \mathbf{B} \rightarrow \Delta}$ $\forall$, r: $\dfrac{\Gamma \rightarrow \mathbf{B}[\mathbf{x} := \mathbf{y}], \Delta}{\Gamma \rightarrow \forall \mathbf{x}\ \mathbf{B}, \Delta}$ $(*b)$

Side-conditions:
$(*b)$ **y** does not occur free in the lower sequent

Figure 3.3. Derivable rules for defined connectives in LKE.

prove something somewhat stronger than that: that whenever we add new rules to the system (as we will do twice later), the LKE rules remain sound, and that if we change the operational semantics at the base of the definition of validity, the LKE rules remain sound. The following theorem proves this.

Theorem 2.1 (Soundness of LKE Rules) If all the premisses of an application of an LKE rule are valid with respect to an operational semantics O and program Π, then so is the conclusion.

Proof : We can analyse each case separately. I will give only representative cases here.

Eq: If an assertion $\mathbf{t} = \mathbf{t}$ appears in the consequent of a sequent, then the sequent is valid, because under any substitution there will be a valid assertion in the consequent, regardless of whether there is a valid assertion in the antecedent.

&, l: Assume that the premiss is valid, and that under a given substitution θ that makes all assertions closed, all the antecedent assertions of the conclusion are valid. Then it must be the case that $\mathbf{B}\theta$ and $\mathbf{C}\theta$ are both valid, so all the antecedent assertions of the premiss are valid under θ; but since the premiss is valid, one of the consequent assertions of the premiss (which is the same as one of the consequent assertions of the conclusion) must be valid under θ as well.

&, r: Assume that the premisses are valid. Under a given substitution θ which makes all the assertions closed, if all the antecedent assertions in either premiss are valid, then so is one of its consequent assertions. If this consequent assertion is one of the Δ assertions, then one of the consequent assertions of the conclusion is also valid under θ. If not, then both $\mathbf{B}\theta$ and $\mathbf{C}\theta$ must be valid, so $(\mathbf{B}\&\mathbf{C})\theta$ must be valid, and again one of the consequent assertions of the conclusion is valid.

$\exists$, l: Assume that the premiss is valid. Let θ be a substitution which makes the conclusion closed; then all substitutions which make the premiss closed will be of the form $\theta[\mathbf{y} := \mathbf{t}]$. Given $\theta[\mathbf{y} := \mathbf{t}]$, there are two possibilities: either one of the assertions in the consequent of the premiss is valid, or one of its antecedent assertions is not valid. In the first case, one of the consequent assertions in the conclusion is valid under θ (since none of the conclusion assertions contain $\mathbf{y}$). In the second case, if the invalid assertion is in the Γ assertions, then there is an invalid assertion in the antecedent of the conclusion as well.

Otherwise, none of the consequent assertions (none of which contain $\mathbf{y}$) are valid under $\theta[\mathbf{y} := \mathbf{t}]$, all the antecedent assertions which do not contain $\mathbf{y}$ are valid under $\theta[\mathbf{y} := \mathbf{t}]$, and $(\mathbf{B}[\mathbf{x} := y])\theta[\mathbf{y} := \mathbf{t}]$ is invalid. But then for the premiss to be valid, $(\mathbf{B}[\mathbf{x} := y])\theta[\mathbf{y} := \mathbf{t}]$ must be invalid for *any* choice of $\mathbf{t}$. This means that for any choice of $\mathbf{t}$, $\mathbf{B}[\mathbf{x} := \mathbf{t}]\theta$ is invalid; $(\exists x\mathbf{B})\theta$ must therefore be invalid, and again there is an invalid assertion in the antecedent of the conclusion.

Sub, r: Under any substitution θ which makes the sequents closed, either $\mathbf{s}$ and $\mathbf{t}$ are not identical (thus making $\mathbf{s} = \mathbf{t}$ invalid and the conclusion valid), or else $\mathbf{s}$ and $\mathbf{t}$ are identical and the two sequents are also identical.

Cut: Assume that the premisses are valid, and that θ makes the sequents closed. If one of the Γ_1 or Γ_2 assertions were invalid under θ, or one of the Δ_1 assertions were valid under θ, the conclusion would be valid under θ. Otherwise, $\mathbf{A}\theta$ must be valid for the first premiss to be valid; but then one of the Δ_2 assertions must be valid for the second premiss to be valid, and again the conclusion is valid under θ.

$\supset, r$: We have the following derivation for this rule. (We treat $\mathbf{B} \supset \mathbf{C}$ as $\neg(\mathbf{B}\&\neg\mathbf{C})$).

$$\cfrac{\cfrac{\cfrac{\Gamma, \mathbf{B} \rightarrow \mathbf{C}, \Delta}{\Gamma, \mathbf{B}, \neg\mathbf{C} \rightarrow \Delta}}{\Gamma, \mathbf{B}\&\neg\mathbf{C} \rightarrow \Delta}}{\Gamma \rightarrow \neg(\mathbf{B}\&\neg\mathbf{C}), \Delta}$$

Other cases are similar. □

I will leave the detailed historical and philosophical discussion of these rules to the end of the chapter, and go on with the technical material.

3. Axioms for Parallel Validity

In this section, I will present and prove valid a set of axioms describing the behaviour, in parallel systems, of the connectives within the S and F signs. These axioms, collectively called PAR, will take the form of sequents. They are intended to be used with the "cut" rule from LKE in the derivation of the success and failure of goal formulae, and in later sections I will prove that this set of laws is complete for this purpose.

The axioms can be seen as distributive laws, because they define how the signs "distribute" over the goal formula connectives. Indeed, the laws for the F signs resemble De Morgan's laws of the distribution of negation over the first order connectives.

3.1. Predicate Unfoldings and the F^N sign

First, some more elucidation of the purpose of the F^N sign is necessary; this will motivate the definition of predicate unfoldings of formulae, which will play an important role in the parallel axioms.

We want to give a "logical" definition of the behaviour of the existential quantifier under failure. In traditional sequent calculi, and in LKE itself, this corresponds to the behaviour of $\exists$ on the left-hand side of a sequent. We would therefore like to be able to assert that $\forall \mathbf{x}\ F(\mathbf{B}) \rightarrow F(\exists \mathbf{x}\ \mathbf{B})$, so that we could (with Cut) replace $F(\exists \mathbf{x}\ \mathbf{B})$ on the right-hand side by $\forall \mathbf{x}\ F(\mathbf{B})$.

However, because of the *Inflist* paradox (page 27), this sequent is not, in fact, valid; there are goal formulae $\mathbf{B}$ such that every instance of $\mathbf{B}$ fails (and thus $\forall \mathbf{x}\ F(\mathbf{B})$ is valid) but $\exists \mathbf{x}\ \mathbf{B}$ diverges.

There are various approaches to a solution to this problem, some of which will be discussed at the end of this chapter. The one followed here is to make a distinction between failure which may involve predicate calls, and failure without predicate calls. The *Inflist* paradox arises because there is no bound to the number of predicate calls that a given instance of $F(Inflist(x))$ can make before failing. The computation of the existential closure essentially tries all possibilities, and thus keeps looking forever. If, however, every instance of a query fails making fewer than a fixed number of predicate calls, then there are only "a finite number of ways" in which instances can fail, so the computation of the existential closure will terminate after trying them all.

We therefore have that $\forall \mathbf{x}\ F^N(\mathbf{B}) \rightarrow F(\exists \mathbf{x}\ \mathbf{B})$ is a valid sequent; if all instances fail without making any predicate calls at all, then the existential closure fails. This rule is not useful for $\mathbf{B}$'s in which the computation *does* involve predicate calls, unless there is some way of converting a query which makes predicate calls into one which does not. Fortunately, because of the way in which we have defined predicate definition, this conversion process can be done easily by expanding predicate calls appearing in the query into their predicate bodies. This is just the familiar "unfolding" operation from Burstall and Darlington [17] or Tamaki and Sato [73]; later, we will meet a different kind of unfolding which is necessary for characterising sequential systems.

Definition 3.1 An assertion (formula) $\mathbf{A}'$ is a *predicate 1-unfolding* of another assertion (formula) $\mathbf{A}$ if it is $\mathbf{A}$ with one occurrence of a subformula $\mathbf{P}(\mathbf{t}_1, \ldots, \mathbf{t}_n)$ replaced by an occurrence of $\mathbf{A}(\mathbf{t}_1, \ldots, \mathbf{t}_n)$, where $\mathbf{P}(\mathbf{x}_1, \ldots, \mathbf{x}_n) \leftrightarrow \mathbf{A}(\mathbf{x}_1, \ldots, \mathbf{x}_n)$ is in the program Π.

$\mathbf{A}'$ is a *predicate unfolding* of $\mathbf{A}$ if it is $\mathbf{A}$ with zero or more successive predicate 1-unfoldings applied to it.

Success axioms:

$S(\ldots)$	left	right
=:	$S(\mathbf{s}=\mathbf{t}) \rightarrow \mathbf{s}=\mathbf{t}$	$\mathbf{s}=\mathbf{t} \rightarrow S(\mathbf{s}=\mathbf{t})$
&:	$S(\mathbf{B}\&\mathbf{C}) \rightarrow S(\mathbf{B})\&S(\mathbf{C})$	$S(\mathbf{B})\&S(\mathbf{C}) \rightarrow S(\mathbf{B}\&\mathbf{C})$
∨:	$S(\mathbf{B} \vee \mathbf{C}) \rightarrow S(\mathbf{B}) \vee S(\mathbf{C})$	$S(\mathbf{B}) \vee S(\mathbf{C}) \rightarrow S(\mathbf{B} \vee \mathbf{C})$
∃:	$S(\exists \mathbf{x}\ \mathbf{B}) \rightarrow \exists \mathbf{x}\ S(\mathbf{B})$	$\exists \mathbf{x}\ S(\mathbf{B}) \rightarrow S(\exists \mathbf{x}\ \mathbf{B})$

Failure axioms:

$F(\ldots)$	left	right
=:	$F(\mathbf{s}=\mathbf{t}) \rightarrow \neg\mathbf{s}=\mathbf{t}$	$\neg\mathbf{s}=\mathbf{t} \rightarrow F(\mathbf{s}=\mathbf{t})$
&:	$F(\mathbf{B}\&\mathbf{C}) \rightarrow F(\mathbf{B}) \vee F(\mathbf{C})$	$F(\mathbf{B}) \vee F(\mathbf{C}) \rightarrow F(\mathbf{B}\&\mathbf{C})$
∨:	$F(\mathbf{B} \vee \mathbf{C}) \rightarrow F(\mathbf{B})\&F(\mathbf{C})$	$F(\mathbf{B})\&F(\mathbf{C}) \rightarrow F(\mathbf{B} \vee \mathbf{C})$
∃:	$F(\exists \mathbf{x}\ \mathbf{B}) \rightarrow \forall \mathbf{x}\ F(\mathbf{B})\ (*a)$	$\forall \mathbf{x}\ F^N(\mathbf{B}) \rightarrow F(\exists \mathbf{x}\ \mathbf{B})$

Miscellaneous axioms:

	left	right
F^N/F^Y:		$F^N(\mathbf{A}) \rightarrow F^Y(\mathbf{A})$
Unf:	$\sigma(\mathbf{A}) \rightarrow \sigma(\mathbf{A}')$	$\sigma(\mathbf{A}') \rightarrow \sigma(\mathbf{A})\ (*b)$
$F^N(\mathbf{P})$:	$F^N(\mathbf{P}(\mathbf{t}_1, \ldots, \mathbf{t}_n)) \rightarrow$	

Notes:
$(*a)$: These rules are asymmetric; all of the other Success and Failure axiom pairs are symmetric.
$(*b)$: Side-condition: $\mathbf{A}'$ is a predicate unfolding of $\mathbf{A}$, and σ is either S or F^Y

Figure 3.4. PAR axioms characterising parallel connectives. F means either F^Y or F^N, its use being consistent throughout each axiom.

In the rules which follow, we will allow the replacement of a formula or assertion by its predicate unfolding and vice versa. The following theorem will help to justify this.

Theorem 3.2 (Operational Equivalence of Predicate Unfoldings) If $\mathbf{A}'$ is a predicate unfolding of $\mathbf{A}$, then any backtrack stack β containing $\mathbf{A}$ succeeds (fails) in any of the SOS variants iff β with $\mathbf{A}$ replaced by $\mathbf{A}'$ succeeds (fails).

Proof: By induction on the number of predicate 1-unfoldings from $\mathbf{A}$ to $\mathbf{A}'$, and on the length of the computation of β. The only non-trivial case is when $\mathbf{A}$ is itself a predicate call, and is the subject of the first step. In this case, it should be clear that a Defined Predicate expansion step can be inserted or deleted to form one computation from the other. □

3.2. The PAR Axioms and their Validity

The laws are in Figure 3.4, presented as a set of axioms, which are in turn just a special kind of rule. We will refer to this set of rules as PAR, since they have to do with the parallel connectives; they are intended to be used in conjunction with the rules from LKE, and we will refer to the combined system as LKE+PAR.

The PAR axioms are in Figure 3.4, classified by the sign involved, the side of the sequent on which we will generally use them, and the connective immediately within the sign. For examples of the use of LKE+PAR to derive sequents, see Appendix A.

As with the LKE rules, we must prove these rules sound – that is, that sequents derivable from valid sequents are also valid. (For brevity, "validity" in this chapter will consistently mean "validity with respect to SOS".)

Theorem 3.3 (Validity of PAR axioms) Each instance of the axiom schemata in PAR is a valid sequent with respect to the operational semantics SOS.

Proof : One case for each arrow direction of each axiom.

$S(=)$: For a given substitution θ which makes the sequent closed, $S(\mathbf{s} = \mathbf{t})$ is valid under θ if and only if $\mathbf{s}\theta$ and $\mathbf{t}\theta$ unify; but since $\mathbf{s}\theta$ and $\mathbf{t}\theta$ are both closed, this happens iff they are identical, that is, iff $\mathbf{s} = \mathbf{t}$ is valid under θ as well.

For the rest of the cases, we will assume that θ is a substitution which makes the sequent closed.

$S(\&)$, left: If $\mathbf{B}\&\mathbf{C}$ succeeds under θ, this must mean that the backtrack stack $(() : \mathbf{B}\theta, \mathbf{C}\theta)$ succeeds. But since both are closed under θ, this can happen only if both succeed independently; that is, if both $S(\mathbf{B})\theta$ and $S(\mathbf{C})\theta$ (and thus $S(\mathbf{B}\&\mathbf{C})\theta$) are valid.

$S(\&)$, right: If $S(\mathbf{B})\&S(\mathbf{C})$ is valid, then both $\mathbf{B}$ and $\mathbf{C}$ must succeed under θ. But then $(() : (\mathbf{B}\&\mathbf{C})\theta)$ will succeed as well, since the success of one closed formula cannot affect the success of another.

$S(\vee)$: $\mathbf{B} \vee \mathbf{C}$ succeeds under θ iff either $\mathbf{B}$ or $\mathbf{C}$ succeed under θ, iff $S(\mathbf{B}) \vee S(\mathbf{C})$ is valid under θ.

$S(\exists)$, left: If $(\exists \mathbf{x}\ \mathbf{B})\theta$ succeeds, there is (by Theorem 5.5) some $\mathbf{t}$ such that $(\mathbf{B}[\mathbf{x} := \mathbf{t}])\theta$ succeeds, so $(\exists \mathbf{x}\ S(\mathbf{B}))\theta$ is valid under θ.

$S(\exists)$, right: From the "one-succeeds-succeeds" theorem (Theorem 5.7).

$F(=)$: $F(\mathbf{s} = \mathbf{t})$ is valid under θ iff $\mathbf{s}\theta$ and $\mathbf{t}\theta$ do not unify; but since $\mathbf{s}\theta$ and $\mathbf{t}\theta$ are both closed, this happens iff they are non-identical, that is, iff $\mathbf{s} = \mathbf{t}$ is invalid (and thus $\neg\mathbf{s} = \mathbf{t}$ is valid) under θ.

$F(\&)$, left: If $\mathbf{B}\&\mathbf{C}$ fails under θ, it must be the case that $(() : \mathbf{B}\theta, \mathbf{C}\theta)$ fails. But since the two formulae share no free variables (because both are closed under θ), this means that one of the two fails independent of the other. So either $\mathbf{B}$ or $\mathbf{C}$ must fail under θ, and $F(\mathbf{B}) \vee F(\mathbf{C})$ is valid under θ. (The same holds if we replace "failure" by "flat failure".)

$F(\&)$, right: If $F(\mathbf{B}) \vee F(\mathbf{C})$ is valid under θ, then either $\mathbf{B}\theta$ or $\mathbf{C}\theta$ must fail; but then $(() : \mathbf{B}\theta, \mathbf{C}\theta)$ must fail too, so $F(\mathbf{B}\&\mathbf{C})\theta$ is valid. (The same holds if we replace "failure" by "failure without predicate calls".)

$F(\vee)$: $\mathbf{B} \vee \mathbf{C}$ fails under θ iff both $\mathbf{B}$ and $\mathbf{C}$ fail under θ, iff $F(\mathbf{B})\&\mathbf{F}(\mathbf{C})$ is valid under θ. (The same holds if we replace "failure" by "flat failure".)

$F(\exists)$, left: There are two subcases, one for F^Y and another for F^N. If $\exists \mathbf{x}\ \mathbf{B}$ fails under θ, then (by Theorem 5.2) $\mathbf{B}[\mathbf{x} := \mathbf{t}]$ fails under θ, for every $\mathbf{t}$; so $\forall \mathbf{x}\ F^Y(\mathbf{B})$ is valid under θ. If $\exists \mathbf{x}\ \mathbf{B}$ fails flatly under θ, then (by reasoning similar to that in the $F(\exists)$, right case) $\mathbf{B}[\mathbf{x} := \mathbf{t}]$ fails flatly under θ; so $\forall \mathbf{x}\ F^N(\mathbf{B})$ is valid under θ.

$F(\exists)$, right: If $\forall \mathbf{x}\ F^N(\mathbf{B})$ is valid under θ, then for all $\mathbf{t}$, the backtrack stack $(() : \mathbf{B}[\mathbf{x} := \mathbf{t}]\theta)$ can fail flatly. Consider the backtrack stack $(() : \mathbf{B}'[\mathbf{x} := \mathbf{t}]\theta$, where $\mathbf{B}'$ is $\mathbf{B}$ with all predicate calls replaced by *true*. This backtrack stack can also fail flatly; therefore it cannot succeed (otherwise it would contradict the Church-Rosser property).

So $(() : \mathbf{B}'[\mathbf{x} := \mathbf{t}]\theta)$ fails for every $\mathbf{t}$; but then the backtrack stack $(() : (\exists \mathbf{x}\ \mathbf{B}')\theta)$ cannot succeed (otherwise it would contradict Theorem 5.5), and it cannot diverge (since it has no predicate calls), so it must fail. Now, the new *true* (i.e., $0 = 0$) subformulae in $\mathbf{B}'$ cannot have any effect on the failure of this backtrack stack, since they have no effect on the substitution in any closure; therefore there is a failing computation which does not perform Unification steps on the *true* subformulae; therefore if these subformulae are replaced by anything, we still get a failing backtrack stack. In particular, the backtrack stack $(() : (\exists \mathbf{x}\ \mathbf{B})\theta)$ must fail flatly.

F^N/F^Y: trivial.

Unf: By Theorem 3.2.

$F^N(\mathbf{P})$: The formula $\mathbf{P}(\mathbf{t}_1, \ldots, \mathbf{t}_n)$ clearly cannot fail without performing Defined Predicate steps, so the sequent as a whole is valid. □

Theorem 3.4 (Soundness of LKE+PAR) Every sequent derivable in LKE+PAR is valid.

Proof : By induction on the structure of the derivation. Cases are from the Validity theorems for LKE and PAR. □

4. Completeness: Closed Assertions

The kinds of completeness results which we can prove of such systems as LKE+PAR tend to fall into groups based on the general approach taken in the proof. One such group is centred around the idea of restricting the places in which free variables can occur, and is the group which we will turn our attention to in this section.

The results in this section and the next are split into a number of stages. This is not because each stage necessarily states an important result, but rather because each stage uses induction over a different measure.

4.1. Completeness for Equality Sequents

I will begin this sequence of results by proving the completeness of LKE for sequents containing only equality formulae. This result will be used in several sections to follow.

Lemma 4.1 Every sequent $\mathcal{S}$ of the form $[\rightarrow \mathbf{s}_1 = \mathbf{t}_1, \ldots, \mathbf{s}_m = \mathbf{t}_m]$, such that there is no i such that $\mathbf{s}_i \equiv \mathbf{t}_i$, is invalid.

Proof : By induction on the measure $j \cdot \omega + k$, where j is the number of free variables in the sequent and k is the number of occurrences of function symbols. When the measure is zero, the sequent is empty and thus invalid. When it is non-zero, we have cases on the form of $\mathcal{S}$.

If there is a formula of the form $\mathbf{f}(\ldots) = \mathbf{g}(\ldots)$ in $\mathcal{S}$, then let $\mathcal{S}'$ be $\mathcal{S}$ without this formula. By the induction hypothesis, $\mathcal{S}'$ is invalid; that is, there is a substitution θ under which all the equalities in $\mathcal{S}'$ are invalid. But since $\mathbf{f}(\ldots) = \mathbf{g}(\ldots)$ is invalid under *any* substitution, all the equalities in $\mathcal{S}$ are invalid under θ as well.

Otherwise, if there is a formula of the form $\mathbf{f}(\mathbf{s}_1, \ldots, \mathbf{s}_n) = \mathbf{f}(\mathbf{t}_1, \ldots, \mathbf{t}_n)$, then since the sequent is invalid, the two terms in the equality must not be identical; so there must be an i such that $\mathbf{s}_i \not\equiv \mathbf{t}_i$. Let $\mathcal{S}'$ be the sequent with this formula replaced by $\mathbf{s}_i = \mathbf{t}_i$. By the induction hypothesis, there is a θ under which all the formulae in $\mathcal{S}'$ are invalid; but then $\mathbf{f}(\mathbf{s}_1, \ldots, \mathbf{s}_n) = \mathbf{f}(\mathbf{t}_1, \ldots, \mathbf{t}_n)$ is clearly invalid under θ as well, and $\mathcal{S}$ is thus also invalid.

Otherwise, all formulae in $\mathcal{S}$ are of the form $\mathbf{x} = \mathbf{t}$ (or its inverse). Consider the variable $\mathbf{x}$ in the first equality. Let $\mathbf{s}_1, \mathbf{s}_2, \mathbf{s}_3, \ldots$ be an infinite sequence of closed terms, and let $i \geq 1$ be such that $\mathbf{x} = \mathbf{s}_i$ does not appear in $\mathcal{S}$. (Note the use of the assumption that we have an infinite number of closed terms; see the discussion at the end of the chapter.) Now let $\mathcal{S}'$ be $\mathcal{S}$ with all occurrences of $\mathbf{x}$ replaced by $\mathbf{s}_i$. $\mathcal{S}'$ has one fewer free variable than $\mathcal{S}$, so by the induction hypothesis, $\mathcal{S}'$ is invalid; that is, there is a substitution θ under which all formulae of $\mathcal{S}'$ are invalid. But this amounts to saying that all formulae of $\mathcal{S}$ are invalid under the substitution $[\mathbf{x} := \mathbf{s}_i]\theta$. □

For the next theorem, we need a short technical lemma to make clear that equality is essentially symmetric under the rules for equality we have given in LKE.

Lemma 4.2 (Symmetry of Equality) The sequent $\mathbf{s} = \mathbf{t} \rightarrow \mathbf{t} = \mathbf{s}$ is derivable in LKE.

Proof : If we take $\mathbf{A}(\mathbf{x})$ to be $\mathbf{x} = \mathbf{s}$, we can use the Sub,r rule of LKE to derive the sequent:

$$\frac{\overline{\mathbf{s} = \mathbf{t} \rightarrow \mathbf{A}(\mathbf{s})}}{\mathbf{s} = \mathbf{t} \rightarrow \mathbf{A}(\mathbf{t})} \qquad i.e. \qquad \frac{\overline{\mathbf{s} = \mathbf{t} \rightarrow \mathbf{s} = \mathbf{s}}}{\mathbf{s} = \mathbf{t} \rightarrow \mathbf{t} = \mathbf{s}}$$

□

Theorem 4.3 (Completeness for Equality) All valid sequents $\mathcal{S}$ containing only equality formulae are derivable in LKE.

Proof : By induction on the measure $j \cdot \omega + k$, where j is the number of free variables in the sequent and k is the number of occurrences of function symbols. When the measure is zero, the sequent is empty and thus invalid, so the result holds trivially.

If there are formulae of the form $\mathbf{f}(\mathbf{s}_1, \ldots, \mathbf{s}_p) = \mathbf{f}(\mathbf{t}_1, \ldots, \mathbf{t}_p)$ in the antecedent, then we can use the Comp rule to produce a sequent which is also valid, but with a lower measure (some of the occurrences of function symbols are gone). By the induction hypothesis, this must be derivable.

Otherwise, if $\mathcal{S}$ is of the form of an Ineq or Occ axiom of LKE, it is clearly derivable.

Otherwise, if there are any formulae in the antecedent at all, they must be of the form $\mathbf{x}_p = \mathbf{t}_p$ (or its inverse – see the Lemma), where $\mathbf{x}_p$ does not occur in $\mathbf{t}_p$. Consider the sequent $\mathcal{S}'$ made from $\mathcal{S}$ by replacing all other occurrences of $\mathbf{x}_1$ by $\mathbf{t}_1$ by running the Sub,l and Sub,r rules backwards, and eliminating $\mathbf{x}_1 = \mathbf{t}_1$ by running the Thin,l rule backwards. Now, if $\mathcal{S}'$ were invalid, it would be because all the antecedent formulae were valid under some θ, but some consequent formula was not. But then $\mathcal{S}$ would be invalid under the substitution $[\mathbf{x} := \mathbf{t}]\theta$ – because the first equality would be valid and the rest of $\mathcal{S}$ would be the same as $\mathcal{S}'$ under θ – contradicting our assumption; so $\mathcal{S}'$ is also valid. $\mathcal{S}'$ is of lower measure than $\mathcal{S}$ because although it may have more occurrences of function symbols, it has one fewer free variable; so by the induction hypothesis, it must be derivable. Since we have constructed $\mathcal{S}'$ by running rules backwards from $\mathcal{S}$, $\mathcal{S}$ is also derivable.

Otherwise, there is an empty antecedent. If there are formulae $\mathbf{s} = \mathbf{s}$ in the consequent, then the sequent is an instance of the Eq axiom from LKE.

Otherwise, by the lemma, the sequent cannot be valid, so the result holds trivially. □

4.2. Closed Completeness

Theorem 4.4 (Closed Completeness, stage 1) All valid sequents $\mathcal{S}$ which have only equalities in the antecedent, and only equalities and F^N formulae in the consequent, are derivable in LKE+PAR.

Proof : By induction on the number of connectives and equality formulae within F^N signs. If this number is 0, then by the Completeness Theorem for Equality, Theorem 4.3, the result holds.

Otherwise, let $\mathcal{S}$ be $\Gamma \rightarrow \Delta, F^N(\mathbf{D}_1), \ldots, F^N(\mathbf{D}_m)$, where the Δ formulae are all equalities. Cases are on $\mathbf{D}_1$. We will derive sequents which must also be valid, and which have fewer connectives and equality formulae within F^N signs.

$\mathbf{D}_1 \equiv (\mathbf{s} = \mathbf{t})$: Assume that $\mathcal{S}$ is valid, and let $\mathcal{S}'$ be $\mathcal{S}$ with $F^N(\mathbf{s} = \mathbf{t})$ taken out of the consequent, and $\mathbf{s} = \mathbf{t}$ put into the antecedent. If $\mathcal{S}'$ were invalid, it would be because there is a θ such that $\mathbf{s}\theta \equiv \mathbf{t}\theta$ but none of $F^N(\mathbf{D}_2)\theta \ldots F^N(\mathbf{D}_m)\theta$ were valid. But then $F^N(\mathbf{s} = \mathbf{t})$ would not be valid under θ either, so $\mathcal{S}$ would be invalid; contradiction. So $\mathcal{S}'$ must be valid; by the induction hypothesis, it is derivable; and $\mathcal{S}$ can be derived from it by an application of the $\neg$, r rule and an application of Cut with the $F(=)$, right axiom from PAR.

$\mathbf{D}_1 \equiv \mathbf{B}\&\mathbf{C}$: Assume that $\mathcal{S}$ is valid, and let $\mathcal{S}'$ be $\mathcal{S}$ with $F^N(\mathbf{B}\&\mathbf{C})$ replaced by $F^N(\mathbf{B}), F^N(\mathbf{C})$. As in the proof of the validity of the $F(\&)$ axioms, $\mathcal{S}'$ must be valid, and $\mathcal{S}$ can be derived from it by $\vee$,r and Cut with $F(\&)$, right.

$\mathbf{D}_1 \equiv \mathbf{B} \vee \mathbf{C}$: Similar to the last case; we can use &,r and $F(\vee)$, right from PAR to derive $\mathcal{S}$ from two valid sequents of lower measure.

$\mathbf{D}_1 \equiv \exists\mathbf{x}\ \mathbf{B}$: Similar to the last two cases; we can use $\forall$,r and $F(\exists)$, right from PAR to derive $\mathcal{S}$ from a valid sequent of lower measure.

Note that $\mathbf{D}_1$ cannot be a predicate application formula because then its failure would inevitably involve a Defined Predicate step. □

In the next stage, we will show completeness for F^Y signed formulae, by showing that we can unfold the formula and then use the F^N/F^Y rule. For this, we need to have the following lemma.

Lemma 4.5 If a backtrack stack β fails, then some predicate unfolding of β can fail without performing any Defined Predicate steps.

Proof : By induction on the number of Defined Predicate steps in the failing computation of β. If this is zero, we already have the result. If it is more than zero, then consider the first Defined Predicate step. The indicated predicate call must be an occurrence of a predicate call which appears in β; let β' be β with that occurrence unfolded. β' has a computation which is identical to that of β, except for one subformula being different and at least one Defined Predicate step being missing (the first one, and possibly later ones resulting from copies of the predicate call being generated by the $\vee$ rule). The result follows from the induction hypothesis. □

Theorem 4.6 (Closed Completeness, stage 2a) All valid sequents $\mathcal{S}$ of the form $[\rightarrow F^Y(\mathbf{A})]$, where $\mathbf{A}$ is a closed formula, are derivable in LKE+PAR.

Proof: $\mathbf{A}$ is a closed formula with a failing computation, so the backtrack stack $((): \mathbf{A})$ fails. By the Lemma, there is therefore some unfolding $\mathbf{A}'$ of $\mathbf{A}$ such that $((): \mathbf{A}')$ fails without Defined Predicate steps. The sequent $[\rightarrow F^N(\mathbf{A}')]$ is therefore valid, and (by the last stage) therefore derivable; $[\rightarrow F^Y(\mathbf{A})]$ is derivable from it by one application of Cut with F^N/F^Y of PAR and zero or more applications of Unf, right of PAR. □

Note that this last proof would not have worked if $\mathbf{A}$ had any free variables, since the lemma does not guarantee that there will be a *single* unfolding which fails without predicate calls for *all* instances of $\mathbf{A}$.

Theorem 4.7 (Closed Completeness, stage 2b) All valid sequents $\mathcal{S}$ of the form $[\rightarrow \mathcal{S}(\mathbf{A})]$, where $\mathbf{A}$ is a closed formula, are derivable in LKE+PAR.

Proof : By the definition of validity, $((): \mathbf{A})$ must succeed. We can proceed by induction on the length of this computation. Cases are on the form of $\mathbf{A}$.

$\mathbf{A} \equiv (\mathbf{s} = \mathbf{t})$: $\mathbf{s}$ and $\mathbf{t}$ are closed, and so must be identical for them to unify. We can therefore derive $\mathcal{S}$ from an Eq axiom and an application of Cut with the $\mathcal{S}(=)$, right axiom of PAR.

$\mathbf{A} \equiv \mathbf{B}\&\mathbf{C}$: $\mathbf{B}$ and $\mathbf{C}$ must succeed independently, each with a shorter computation than $\mathbf{B}\&\mathbf{C}$. $\mathcal{S}$ must therefore be derivable from $[\rightarrow \mathcal{S}(\mathbf{B})]$ and $[\rightarrow \mathcal{S}(\mathbf{C})]$ by &,r and Cut with $\mathcal{S}(\&)$, right of PAR.

$\mathbf{A} \equiv \mathbf{B} \vee \mathbf{C}$: The first step of the successful computation of $\mathbf{B} \vee \mathbf{C}$ must be to split the closure into two on the backtrack stack. By Lemma 3.4, either the backtrack stack $((): \mathbf{B})$ or the backtrack stack $((): \mathbf{C})$ must succeed; therefore, by the induction hypothesis either $[\rightarrow \mathcal{S}(\mathbf{B})]$ or $[\rightarrow \mathcal{S}(\mathbf{C})]$ must be derivable. We can derive $\mathcal{S}$ from the derivable one by applications of Thin,r and $\vee$,r and Cut with $\mathcal{S}(\vee)$, right from PAR.

$\mathbf{A} \equiv \exists \mathbf{x}\ \mathbf{B}$: By the "succeeds-one-succeeds" theorem (Theorem 5.5), there must be a closed $\mathbf{t}$ such that $\mathbf{B}[\mathbf{x} := \mathbf{t}]$ succeeds, and it must do so with a computation with at least one step fewer than that of $\exists \mathbf{x}\ \mathbf{B}$. By the induction hypothesis, therefore, $[\rightarrow \mathcal{S}(\mathbf{B}[\mathbf{x} := \mathbf{t}])]$ must be derivable; and $\mathcal{S}$ is derivable from it by $\exists$,r and Cut with $\mathcal{S}(\exists)$, right of PAR.

$\mathbf{A} \equiv \mathbf{P}(\mathbf{t}_1, \ldots, \mathbf{t}_n)$: The successful computation must start with a Defined Predicate step, and so the predicate 1-unfolding of $\mathbf{A}$ must have a shorter computation than $\mathbf{A}$. $\mathcal{S}$ is therefore derivable by Cut with Unf, right of PAR. □

Theorem 4.8 (Closed Completeness, stage 3) All valid sequents $\mathcal{S}$ which have only equalities in the antecedent, and only equalities and signed formulae in the consequent, and where no free variable appears in any S or F^Y assertion, are derivable in LKE+PAR.

Proof : If some S or F^Y assertion in the consequent is valid, we can derive $\mathcal{S}$ by thinning out all other assertions (by stages 2a and 2b). Otherwise, none of the S or F^Y assertions can be valid under any substitution (since they are closed); so those assertions can be thinned out and the remaining sequent is derivable (by stage 1). □

In the last stage, we will generalise the third stage in the direction of permitting arbitrary assertions in sequents. However, we still cannot handle signed formulae in the antecedent at the base of the induction, so we must ban them from any context where they will end up in the antecedent. (But see the discussion on guaranteed-terminating queries, below.) This leads to the standard concept of "positive" and "negative" contexts.

Definition 4.9 An occurrence of a term, formula, signed formula, or assertion appears *in a positive context* in a sequent if it appears within an even number of negations in the consequent, or within an odd number of negations in the antecedent. It appears *in a negative context* in a sequent if it appears within an odd number of negations in the consequent, or within an even number of negations in the antecedent.

Theorem 4.10 (Closed Completeness, stage 4) All valid sequents $\mathcal{S}$ in which no free variable appears in an S or F^Y subassertion, and no signed formula appears in a negative context, are derivable in LKE+PAR.

Proof : By induction on the total number n of connectives outside signed formulae. $n = 0$ is the previous stage. For $n > 0$, we have cases on the first connective; these cases follow straightforwardly from the induction hypothesis, except for the case of an existential quantifier $(\exists \mathbf{x}\ \mathbf{B})$ on the left.

In that case, let $\mathcal{S}'$ be the premiss of an application of the $\exists$,l rule of which $\mathcal{S}$ is the conclusion. If $\mathcal{S}'$ were invalid, it would be because under some θ, all of its antecedent assertions but none of its consequent assertions are valid. But if $\mathbf{B}[\mathbf{x} := \mathbf{y}]\theta$ is valid, then $(\exists \mathbf{x}\ \mathbf{B})\theta$ must be valid (since whatever θ substitutes for $\mathbf{y}$ is a witness for $\mathbf{x}$); but then $\mathcal{S}$ would be invalid, since under θ all of *its* antecedent assertions and none of its consequent assertions are valid; contradiction. Therefore $\mathcal{S}'$ must be valid, and by the induction hypothesis is derivable; so $\mathcal{S}$ is derivable as well. □

Some examples of sequents which are valid but underivable in LKE+PAR are $[\rightarrow S(Add(x, 0, x))]$, where *Add* is the familiar addition predicate for Peano integers (underivable because it has a free variable), and $[S(Loop()) \rightarrow]$, where *Loop* is the infinite loop predicate (valid because the assumption that *Loop*() succeeds is false, but underivable because the expansion of *Loop*() goes on forever). We will look at ways in which these sources of incompleteness can be handled in Chapter 5.

There are also sequents which are valid *and* derivable, but not covered by the Closed Completeness results here; one example is $[F(\mathbf{s} = \mathbf{s}) \rightarrow]$. This sequent will fall into a class of sequents to be proven derivable in Section 5. below, but in general it seems difficult to describe natural and useful classes of valid, derivable sequents. The class described in Closed Completeness, stage 4 and the class described in Section 5. are two of the most natural.

Note that because of the restrictions on the class of valid sequents being proved derivable, the left-hand rules of PAR were never used in the completeness proof. They will be used in the proofs in Section 5..

4.3. Characterisation Results

The results in this section avoid the *negative* results about incompleteness discussed in Chapter 5. However, this incompleteness arises in part because of the great expressive power of sequents. We have already effectively characterised the classes of queries which succeed or fail in a system with parallel connectives. Here, therefore, are the main *positive* results arising from the completeness theorems; they are some of the most important results in the thesis.

Theorem 4.11 (Characterisation of SOS) A goal formula $\mathbf{A}$ succeeds in SOS iff the sequent $[\rightarrow S(\exists[\mathbf{A}])]$ is derivable in LKE+PAR; it fails in SOS iff the sequent

$[\rightarrow F^Y(\exists[\mathbf{A}])]$ is derivable in LKE+PAR.

Proof: First note that $\mathbf{A}$ succeeds (fails) iff $\exists[\mathbf{A}]$, its existential closure, succeeds (fails); this is because the backtrack stack $(() : \exists[\mathbf{A}])$ must be computed by first doing one $\exists$ step for each quantified variable. The rest of the theorem follows from the Soundness theorem for LKE+PAR and the Closed Completeness, stage 3 theorem. □

What this means is that we have succeeded in logically characterising the two outer circles of the Venn diagram, Figure 2.6. A query $\mathbf{A}$ is in the outer failure set iff $[\rightarrow F^Y(\exists[\mathbf{A}])]$ is derivable, and it is in the outer success set iff $[\rightarrow S(\exists[\mathbf{A}])]$ is derivable. Because of the great expressive power of sequents, sequents can express many more things than just the success or failure of individual queries; the incompleteness of LKE+PAR is only in these areas.

LKE+PAR has enabled us to achieve one part of our main goal: the logical characterisation of the sets of queries which succeed or fail in the parallel operational semantics SOS. Because of the completeness properties of SOS/so and SOS/sa, we have also characterised the queries which fail in SOS/so and those which succeed in SOS/sa.

5. Completeness: Predicate-Free Assertions

Another group of completeness results for LKE+PAR is centred around the idea of disallowing defined predicate formulae in assertions. This restriction can be lifted if we restrict the program to one having no definitions of recursive or mutually-recursive predicates.

Such restrictions are very severe from a logic programming standpoint. In this group, however, there is no restriction on where signed formulae can appear, and no restriction on free variables (unlike the group in the last section). This tends to suggest that, to some degree, it is the interaction between free variables and recursive predicates which causes the lack of a complete proof system.

Theorem 5.1 (Flat Completeness, stage 1) All valid sequents $\mathcal{S}$ containing no signed formulae are derivable in LKE.

Proof: By induction on the number of connectives in $\mathcal{S}$. The case 0 is the Completeness for Equality theorem. When there are connectives, we can eliminate each one with one application of an LKE rule, to form a sequent which is also valid but with a lower number of connectives. Cases are straightforward, except for the $\exists$,l case, which is similar to the reasoning in the Closed Completeness, stage 4 theorem. □

Theorem 5.2 (Flat Completeness, stage 2) All valid sequents $\mathcal{S}$ containing no predicate calls are derivable in LKE+PAR.

Proof: By induction on $j{\cdot}\omega{+}k$, where j is the total number of connectives within signed formulae, and k is the total number of connectives anywhere in assertions containing signed formulae. Case 0 is the previous stage (no assertions contain signed formulae). If there are assertions containing signed formulae, we have cases on the first such formula in the sequent.

If this formula is not itself a signed formula, we can eliminate its top-level connective in the manner of the last stage, decreasing k by one. (In the rest of the cases, we will push one connective outside the sign of a signed formula, leaving k the same but decreasing j by one.)

Otherwise, it is a signed formula. If it is of the form $S(\mathbf{s} = \mathbf{t})$, then let $\mathcal{S}'$ be $\mathcal{S}$ with this assertion replaced by $\mathbf{s} = \mathbf{t}$. By the validity of the PAR axiom $S(=)$,l, $\mathcal{S}'$ is valid; we can derive $\mathcal{S}$ from it by an application of Cut with $S(=)$,r. The same reasoning holds for the other $S(\mathbf{A})$ assertions, $F(=)$, $F(\&)$, $F(\vee)$, and $F^N(\exists)$. It does not hold for $F^Y(\exists)$ because there is a different rule for each direction.

If the signed formula is of the form $F^Y(\exists\mathbf{x}\mathbf{B})$ and is in the antecedent, then let $\mathcal{S}'$ be $\mathcal{S}$ with this assertion replaced by $\forall\mathbf{x}F^Y(\mathbf{B})$. $\mathcal{S}$ can be derived from $\mathcal{S}'$ by Cut with $F(\exists)$,l; we now need only to show that $\mathcal{S}'$ is valid. Let $\mathcal{S}''$ be $\mathcal{S}$ with $F^Y(\exists\mathbf{x}\mathbf{B})$ replaced by $\forall\mathbf{x}F^N(\mathbf{B})$. $\mathcal{S}''$ is derivable from $\mathcal{S}$ (by Cut with $F(\exists)$,r), and so must be valid; but since $\mathbf{B}$ contains no predicate calls, $F^Y(\mathbf{B})$ implies that $F^N(\mathbf{B})$, and $\mathcal{S}'$ is also valid.

If the signed formula is of the form $F^Y(\exists\mathbf{x}\mathbf{B})$ and is in the consequent, then let $\mathcal{S}'$ be $\mathcal{S}$ with this assertion replaced by $\forall\mathbf{x}F^N(\mathbf{B})$. $\mathcal{S}$ can be derived from $\mathcal{S}'$ by Cut with $F(\exists)$,r and F^N/F^Y from PAR; but $\mathcal{S}'$ can be derived from $\mathcal{S}$ by Cut with $F(\exists)$,l, and so must be valid. □

This last stage says that as long as we restrict our attention to only predicate-free sequents, we can prove any valid sequent. This is not very useful for characterising logic programming, since there we are mostly concerned with proving properties of recursive predicates. Its utility is mainly in casting light on the question of why there is no complete proof system.

One way of strengthening this result is to allow predicate calls, but to disallow recursion in the base program. This kind of result suggests that it is not exactly predicate calls, but calls to recursive predicates that causes the problem.

Definition 5.3 A *hierarchical* program Π is one in which each predicate $\mathbf{P}$ in the language $\mathcal{L}$ can be assigned a natural number $n_{\mathbf{P}} > 0$ such that if $\mathbf{P}$ calls $\mathbf{Q}$ as defined in Π, $n_{\mathbf{Q}} < n_{\mathbf{P}}$.

Theorem 5.4 If Π is hierarchical, then all valid sequents $\mathcal{S}$ are derivable in LKE+PAR.

Proof : By the techniques of this section, except that signed formulae containing predicate calls are expanded by a finite number of applications of Cut with Unf from PAR. □

There are various ways in which we could combine the results of the last section with those of this section, to describe wider and wider classes of sequents or programs for which LKE+PAR is complete. Unfortunately, these classes are somewhat unnatural and difficult to describe. Here are some brief examples.

Theorem 5.5 All valid sequents in which no predicate calls appear in a negative context, and no S or F^Y formula in a positive context contains both predicate calls and free variables, are derivable in LKE+PAR.

Proof : We can eliminate S and F^Y signed formulae containing no predicate calls by the method of the last theorem. After that, the sequent will be in the form of the Closed Completeness, stage 4 theorem of the last section. □

Another example is that we could replace the restriction to hierarchical programs by a restriction that only hierarchical predicates within programs can appear in the antecedent. This is not much of a relaxation, because typically, many of the most useful predicates in programs are recursive.

6. Discussion

Here I present some notes of a more philosophical and historical nature on the contents of this chapter, which would have seemed out of place in the technical discussions earlier.

6.1. LKE

Equality has been examined in the context of first order logic for decades. Commentators such as Fitch [32] and Church [20] give axiomatisations for simple equality between first order terms, and note that the axiom $\forall x(x = x)$ and some form of substitution axiom schemata are sufficient to deduce the transitivity and symmetry of equality. Takeuti [72] casts this into sequent calculus form by augmenting Gentzen's LK [36] to a calculus LK_e; this calculus has the property that a sequent is derivable in it iff the sequent with the equality axioms added to the antecedent is derivable.

The notion of validity associated with these formalisations of equality leaves open the possibility that two non-identical closed terms might be equal. For the purposes of logic programming, we want to exclude this possibility. We thus want an axiomatisation equivalent to Clark's equality theory [22]; actually, any sequent calculus which has the completeness property for equality between closed terms as syntactic identity, will do for this purpose. LKE is simply Gentzen's LK with such additional axioms and rules.

Readers might be curious about the classical nature of LKE. Recent results [54] show that logic programming has a strong connection with intuitionistic logic, but LKE is clearly a classical sequent calculus. However, these results are about the internal logic within logic programming, and in LKE+PAR we are concerned with notions of proving properties of success and failure of queries in a program logic.

Constructivist principles should not bar us from working classically in this setting, because given our definition of validity, the law of excluded middle clearly holds for all assertions. Note, for instance, that no predicates other than equality can appear at the top level of sequents, and that all other predicate applications are enclosed within signs.

6.2. PAR

The classicality of the assertion connectives is exploited in the PAR axioms, which present in a clear and concise manner the relationship between goal formula connectives *within* signed formulae and assertion connectives *outside* signed formulae. The S axioms state that success of a query is essentially the same as its provability in LKE (given the expansion of predicates with the Unfolding rule). The F axioms, like De Morgan's laws, state how failure can be "pushed down through" the goal formula connectives, converting conjunctions into disjunctions, disjunctions into conjunctions, and existentials into universals.

The only elements which mar the compositionality of the PAR axioms are the F^N/F^Y dichotomy and the associated unfolding of predicate calls within goal formulae. This device is necessitated by the inherent asymmetry in logic programming discussed in Chapter

2: essentially, we terminate if only one solution is found, but rather than terminating if only one counterexample is found, we keep discarding counterexamples until we are satisfied that every element of the domain is a counterexample.

6.3. Characterising Success Alone

If we had not wanted to characterise failure in the calculus, we would have been able to simplify it considerably. One simple presentation of the calculus is as follows.

Let predicate application formulae also be assertions. Let the definition of validity with respect to Π make no mention of failure, but include a clause to the effect that closed formulae of the form $\mathbf{P}(\mathbf{t}_1, \ldots, \mathbf{t}_n)$ are valid if the corresponding $\mathbf{A}(\mathbf{t}_1, \ldots, \mathbf{t}_n)$ formula is valid.

Let the axioms PAR′ be the two axioms $S(\mathbf{A}) \rightarrow \mathbf{A}$ and $\mathbf{A} \rightarrow S(\mathbf{A})$. We can prove every closed instance of these axioms valid by induction on the length of the computation of $\mathbf{A}$ and on the stage of the inductive definition of validity at which $\mathbf{A}$ becomes valid. (In fact, in this formulation, the sign S has no significance other than to mark a goal formula, and can be done away with.)

Now consider the set of axioms DEF_Π formed from the program Π, and consisting of an axiom of the form $\mathbf{P}(\mathbf{t}_1, \ldots, \mathbf{t}_n) \rightarrow \mathbf{A}(\mathbf{t}_1, \ldots, \mathbf{t}_n)$ and one of the form $\mathbf{A}(\mathbf{t}_1, \ldots, \mathbf{t}_n) \rightarrow \mathbf{P}(\mathbf{t}_1, \ldots, \mathbf{t}_n)$ for every predicate defined in Π. These axioms are trivially valid.

The Closed Completeness and Flat Completeness results of this chapter now hold for LKE+DEF_Π+PAR′: we can replace $S(\mathbf{A})$ by $\mathbf{A}$ in any sequent to obtain a sequent which is also valid, and LKE+DEF_Π is complete for the new definition of validity.

This line of development is similar in spirit to that of Hagiya and Sakurai [41] and Hallnäs and Schroeder-Heister [42]. When we move to expand this calculus to take account of failure, however, we need the concepts of flat failure and predicate unfolding. The predicate unfolding rule extends easily to successful formulae, and thus does away with the need to take account of predicate calls at the top level of sequents.

As we will see in the next chapter, in the context of sequential computation, we need to characterise failure in order to characterise success, so the two signs are necessary from the start. The presentation of LKE+PAR in this chapter is therefore more in harmony with the calculus in the next chapter than is the simpler characterisation I just gave.

6.4. More Practical Failure Rules

Implicit in the completeness theorems is a method for finding a derivation for $[\rightarrow F^Y(\exists \mathbf{x}\ \mathbf{B})]$ sequents: unfold occurrences of predicate calls in $\mathbf{B}$ to the required depth, and then use the other rules. This is sufficient for the purpose of proving the theorems, but might be too clumsy for practical use.

An alternative formulation would have the F^N sign replaced by an infinite number of signs F^n, where $n \geq 0$ is the number of Defined Predicate steps allowed in the failing computation. The definition of validity would be changed accordingly. We would then have that $\forall \mathbf{x} F^n(\mathbf{B}) \rightarrow F^Y(\exists \mathbf{x} \mathbf{B})$ for any n, and the Unfolding axioms could simply take the following forms:

$\sigma(\mathbf{A}(\mathbf{t}_1, \ldots, \mathbf{t}_n)) \rightarrow \sigma(\mathbf{P}(\mathbf{t}_1, \ldots, \mathbf{t}_n))$; $\sigma(\mathbf{P}(\mathbf{t}_1, \ldots, \mathbf{t}_n)) \rightarrow \sigma(\mathbf{A}(\mathbf{t}_1, \ldots, \mathbf{t}_n))$
where σ is S or F^Y, and $\mathbf{P}(\mathbf{x}_1, \ldots, \mathbf{x}_n) \leftrightarrow \mathbf{A}(\mathbf{x}_1, \ldots, \mathbf{x}_n)$ is in the program Π;
$F^n(\mathbf{A}(\mathbf{t}_1, \ldots, \mathbf{t}_n)) \rightarrow F^{n+1}(\mathbf{P}(\mathbf{t}_1, \ldots, \mathbf{t}_n))$,

$F^{n+1}(\mathbf{P}(\mathbf{t}_1, \ldots, \mathbf{t}_n)) \rightarrow F^n(\mathbf{A}(\mathbf{t}_1, \ldots, \mathbf{t}_n))$
where $\mathbf{P}(\mathbf{x}_1, \ldots, \mathbf{x}_n) \leftrightarrow \mathbf{A}(\mathbf{x}_1, \ldots, \mathbf{x}_n)$ is in the program Π.
We would then be able to delay the unfolding of predicate calls later, until it became clear that the unfolding was needed; the choice of n in the application of the F^n/F^Y rule would be left to the user, who might be able to make a good guess on a convenient number. I avoided this formulation only because it would have unnecessarily complicated some of the proofs, for no mathematical gain.

A related idea is to have the validity of an assertion be relative to a fixed bound on how many predicate expansions an F^N formula is allowed to make. We would define *k-validity* of closed assertions as identical to validity, except that $F^N(\mathbf{A})$ would be k-valid iff $\mathbf{A}$ failed performing k predicate expansions or fewer. We would then define validity for sequents as follows: a sequent is valid iff there is a k such that for all θ, if all the antecedent formulae are valid under θ, then one of the consequent formulae is valid under θ. The PAR rules would change as in the last paragraph. Again, although this might be more practically convenient, I have avoided this formulation due to its unnecessary complexity.

Chapter 4

Characterising Sequential Systems

In this chapter, I will give a characterisation of the two inner circles of the Venn diagram in Figure 2.6 in the same way as I characterised the two outer circles. That is, I will give a proof-theoretic characterisation of sequential logic programming (in particular, the operational semantics SP) in the form of a sequent calculus.

For this sequent calculus, we can use the rules LKE from the last chapter unchanged; we need only give a new group of axioms, SEQ, corresponding to PAR from the last chapter. These axioms, however, are more complex than those in PAR, have more side-conditions, and in particular involve the concept of *disjunctive unfoldings* of formulae.

Nevertheless, we can prove the same things about SEQ that we can about PAR: the laws are sound, and the proof system LKE+SEQ characterises sequential logic programming in several useful ways.

I will also give a characterisation of the last circle in Figure 2.6, namely the middle success circle. This set contains all queries which succeed in SOS/so, and can be characterised by a set of axioms, PASO, which combines axioms from PAR and from SEQ in a simple and intuitively clear way.

1. Approaches to Semantics

I begin by going into more detail about why we want a semantics for sequential logic programming, and what approaches have been taken so far to giving one.

The assumptions made about search strategies in most research on foundations of logic programming (for instance, SLD-resolution with a fair search rule) are not satisfied by sequential logic programming. Sequential Prolog systems may diverge in cases where fair SLD-resolution can succeed, or in cases where parallel Prologs can fail.

However, it seems clear that sequential Prolog is a useful language – and thus needs a mathematical semantics which will allow us to do such things as proving termination and correctness properties of programs. Various approaches have been taken to describing termination and correctness, including analyses of the operational semantics, and denotational descriptions that implicitly take termination into account.

1.1. Operational Approaches

In a paper of Francez et al. [34], a characterisation is given of terminating Prolog computations in terms of operational semantics. One can prove that a computation terminates by giving conditions on the form of the tree of candidate solutions: if there are no infinite branches to the left of the first solution, then the program terminates. Francez et al. also give a proof system in which proofs of properties of programs can be made.

This is an adequate method of characterising termination. However, the operational semantics of a logic programming language is clearly secondary to the declarative semantics, which is where the whole purpose of the language comes from. A characterisation of termination in terms of the underlying logic of the language would be preferable to this purely operational description. Their proof system approach, while having a logical structure, reifies such concepts as answer substitutions and unification, which are more properly of the operational semantics than the abstract logical structure of Prolog programs. We therefore achieve very little abstract mathematical insight from this technique.

1.2. Denotational Approaches

There have been several denotational analyses of sequential Prolog (some examples are [48, 9, 27, 12, 26, 57]), and these seem to bring out deeper and more abstract properties of the language.

Of these, one appealing example is Baudinet's [12]. In this semantics, queries are given denotations in the set of functions which map substitutions to (essentially) sequences of substitutions. "Append" and "join" operators are defined which allow the derivation of denotations of composite goals, and of sequences of clauses, from the denotations of individual atoms. This semantics is therefore compositional and has clear connections to standard techniques in denotational semantics.

However, it is disappointing that this characterisation is so functional and so far removed from logic. Unification is again reified, and the result of a computation is viewed as the result of a composition of functions applied to the empty substitution. One might argue that this kind of functional denotational semantics is inappropriate for logic programming for philosophical reasons: denotational semantics views every program as a function from inputs to outputs, while the whole point of the logic programming paradigm is that it is not necessary to view a program in this way. The reason that programmers choose a logic programming language is often that their problem has some inherent logical structure which is reflected in the language, and not well described by functions.

One advantage of denotational semantics approaches like Baudinet's is that they allow a description of cut and negation as failure which is well-integrated with the rest of the semantics. The well-known "non-logical" nature of these features remains, however.

2. Disjunctive Unfoldings

The notion of the disjunctive unfolding of a formula is one of the main novelties of this thesis, and the mechanism which allows us to isolate the non-compositionality of sequential Prolog. The disjunctive unfolding of a formula $\mathbf{A}$ is a formula $\mathbf{A}'$ which is classically equivalent to $\mathbf{A}$, but has the property that its satisfiability depends only on the satisfiability of its subformulae.

This requires some motivation. Once we have set out to develop a proof system characterising sequential Prolog, there is one fairly natural way to proceed (which has been followed independently, for example, by Girard [38]). However, the resulting proof system still has soundness problems; as with full first order logic, we can still prove things which have no corresponding computation.

Unfoldings of formulae are exactly what we need to solve these soundness problems. This section will present the idea of unfoldings by giving an outline of the initial attempt at a proof system, describing that system's problems, defining the predicate and disjunctive unfoldings of a formula, and proving some essential properties of unfoldings.

2.1. An Initial Attempt at a Characterisation

We would like to give axioms which characterise sequential logic programming as the PAR axioms characterise parallel logic programming. For instance, in sequential logic programming, **B**&**C** succeeds if both **B** and **C** succeed, and **B**&**C** fails if either **B** fails, or **B** succeeds and **C** fails. We might imagine that the axioms for success and failure of conjunctions would therefore be something like the following:

$S(\&)$: $\dfrac{}{S(\mathbf{B}\&\mathbf{C}) \leftrightarrow S(\mathbf{B})\&S(\mathbf{C})}$ $F(\&)$: $\dfrac{}{F(\mathbf{B}\&\mathbf{C}) \leftrightarrow F(\mathbf{B}) \vee (S(\mathbf{B})\&F(\mathbf{C}))}$

The axioms for success and failure of disjunctions would presumably be the duals of these:

$S(\vee)$: $\dfrac{}{S(\mathbf{B} \vee \mathbf{C}) \leftrightarrow S(\mathbf{B}) \vee (F(\mathbf{B})\&S(\mathbf{C}))}$ $F(\vee)$: $\dfrac{}{F(\mathbf{B} \vee \mathbf{C}) \leftrightarrow F(\mathbf{B})\&F(\mathbf{C})}$

However, although the $\rightarrow$ direction of these axioms are sound, the $\leftarrow$ direction of the $F(\&)$ axiom – the direction we need to prove sequents of the form $[\rightarrow\ F(\mathbf{B}\&\mathbf{C})]$ – is not sound. Consider the query $(true \vee Loop())\&false$. This query diverges according to the operational semantics SP; the transitions are
$(() : (true \vee Loop())\&false) \stackrel{SP}{\Rightarrow} (() : true \vee Loop(), false) \stackrel{SP}{\Rightarrow}$
$(() : true, false); (() : Loop(), false) \stackrel{SP}{\Rightarrow} (() : false); (() : Loop(), false) \stackrel{SP}{\Rightarrow}$
$(() : Loop(), false) \stackrel{SP}{\Rightarrow} (() : Loop(), false) \stackrel{SP}{\Rightarrow} \ldots$
However, with the rules given above, we can "prove" that it fails.

$$\dfrac{\dfrac{\dfrac{\dfrac{\dfrac{}{\rightarrow 0=0, F(true)\&S(Loop())}}{\rightarrow S(true), F(true)\&S(Loop())}}{\rightarrow S(true) \vee (F(true)\&S(Loop()))}}{\rightarrow S(true \vee Loop())} \qquad \dfrac{\dfrac{\dfrac{}{0=1 \rightarrow}}{\rightarrow \neg(0=1)}}{\rightarrow F(false)}}{\dfrac{\dfrac{\dfrac{\rightarrow S(true \vee Loop())\&F(false)}{\rightarrow F(true \vee Loop()), S(true \vee Loop())\&F(false)}}{\rightarrow F(true \vee Loop()) \vee (S(true \vee Loop())\&F(false))}}{\rightarrow F((true \vee Loop())\&false)}}$$

But now consider the query $(true\&false) \vee (Loop()\&false)$. This is classically equivalent to the previous query, and is handled in much the same way by the operational semantics SP; in fact, the computation is exactly the same after one steps. However, we cannot get a derivation of $[\rightarrow\ F((true\&false) \vee (Loop()\&false))]$; in other words, the proof system behaves *correctly* in regard to this query.

Basically, if a query has all its disjunctions outside all its conjunctions and existential quantifiers, then it will be handled correctly by the simple proof rules above. Many queries will not have this property. However, a query can be transformed in this direction

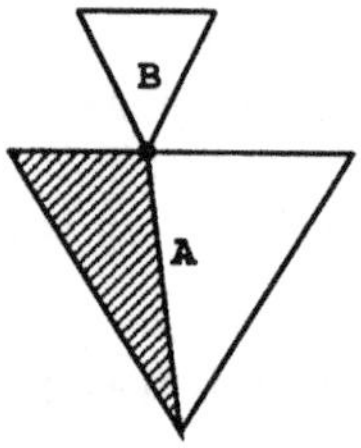

Figure 4.1. **B** is the key subformula of formula **A**. Informally, the shaded region consists only of =, &, and ∃ formulae.

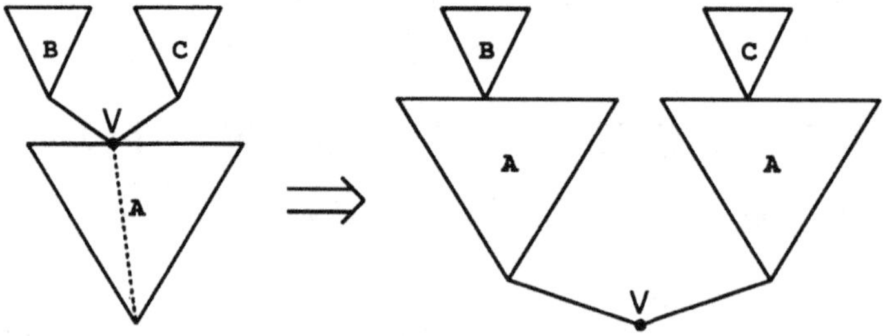

Figure 4.2. Disjunctive unfolding of a formula. The indicated disjunction, $\mathbf{B} \vee \mathbf{C}$, is the key subformula of **A**.

by taking the first disjunction encountered in a depth-first traversal of the formula, and "pulling it toward the outside of the formula" by distributing the conjunctions and quantifiers over it. There is the added complication that disjunctions may be "hidden" inside predicate calls, but this can be handled by expanding predicate calls.

2.2. Definitions and Examples

The above discussion motivates the following definitions.

Definition 2.1 The *key subformula* of a formula is the leftmost disjunction or predicate application subformula which is not a proper subformula of another disjunction. (See Figure 4.1.) Not every formula has a key subformula.

The *disjunctive unfolding* of a formula **A** with key subformula $\mathbf{B} \vee \mathbf{C}$ is the formula $\mathbf{A}^{\mathbf{B}} \vee \mathbf{A}^{\mathbf{C}}$, where $\mathbf{A}^{\mathbf{B}}$ (resp. $\mathbf{A}^{\mathbf{C}}$) means **A** with its key subformula replaced by **B** (resp. **C**). (See Figure 4.2.) Formulae which do not have a disjunctive key subformula have no disjunctive unfolding; we write $\mathbf{A} \stackrel{\mathrm{Disj}}{\Rightarrow} \mathbf{A}'$ if $\mathbf{A}'$ is the disjunctive unfolding of **A**.

Examples. The formulae $(\mathbf{B} \vee \mathbf{C})\&\mathbf{s} = \mathbf{t}$, $\exists x(\mathbf{s} = \mathbf{t}\&(\mathbf{B} \vee \mathbf{C}))$, and $\mathbf{B} \vee \mathbf{C}$ all have $\mathbf{B} \vee \mathbf{C}$ as their key subformulae. The disjunctive unfoldings of these formulae are, respectively, $(\mathbf{B}\&\mathbf{s} = \mathbf{t}) \vee (\mathbf{C}\&\mathbf{s} = \mathbf{t})$; $\exists x(\mathbf{s} = \mathbf{t}\&\mathbf{B}) \vee \exists x(\mathbf{s} = \mathbf{t}\&\mathbf{C})$; and $\mathbf{B} \vee \mathbf{C}$ itself. The formula $\mathbf{P}(x)\&(\mathbf{B} \vee \mathbf{C})$ has $\mathbf{P}(x)$ as its key subformula; the formula $\exists x(x = 0\&x = 1)$ has no key subformula.

As we will see in future sections, we can make the simple proof rules given in section 2.1. work properly if we first restrict certain formulae in the rules to be formulae without predicate application subformulae, and then add a rule allowing a formula to be transformed by a disjunctive unfolding as well as a predicate unfolding.

2.3. Some Facts about Unfoldings

For now, we must show that the disjunctive unfolding of a formula, like predicate unfoldings, are equivalent to that formula under the operational semantics. This fact will be important for proving the soundness and completeness results to come. Unfortunately, this proof is not as straightforward as that for predicate unfoldings, and involves a long case analysis.

Theorem 2.2 (Operational Equivalence of Disjunctive Unfoldings) If $\mathbf{A} \overset{\mathrm{Disj}}{\Rightarrow} \mathbf{A}'$, then $(\theta : \mathbf{A}, \alpha); \beta$ succeeds (fails) in SP iff $(\theta : \mathbf{A}', \alpha); \beta$ succeeds (fails) in SP.

Proof : ($\rightarrow$) By induction on the depth of the key subformula (which is a disjunction) in the tree of the formula **A**. In what follows, I use the notation $\beta \overset{\mathrm{SP}*}{\Rightarrow} S/F$ to denote that β succeeds or fails, its meaning being consistent through the analysis of each case.

Case depth = 0: **A** is itself a disjunction, so its disjunctive unfolding is itself. The result holds trivially.

Case depth > 0: **A** can be either a conjunction or an existential formula.

- $\mathbf{A} \equiv \mathbf{B}\&\mathbf{C}$. We have the computation

$$(\theta : \mathbf{B}\&\mathbf{C}, \alpha); \beta \overset{\mathrm{SP}}{\Rightarrow} (\theta : \mathbf{B}, \mathbf{C}, \alpha); \beta \overset{\mathrm{SP}*}{\Rightarrow} S/F$$

  There are two subcases to consider.

  - The key subformula, $\mathbf{B}_1 \vee \mathbf{B}_2$, is in **B**. The disjunctive unfolding of **B** is therefore $\mathbf{B}^{\mathbf{B}_1} \vee \mathbf{B}^{\mathbf{B}_2}$, and $\mathbf{A}'$ is $(\mathbf{B}^{\mathbf{B}_1}\&\mathbf{C}) \vee (\mathbf{B}^{\mathbf{B}_2}\&\mathbf{C})$. By the induction hypothesis, we have that

$$(\theta : \mathbf{B}^{\mathbf{B}_1} \vee \mathbf{B}^{\mathbf{B}_2}, \mathbf{C}, \alpha); \beta \overset{\mathrm{SP}}{\Rightarrow} (\theta : \mathbf{B}^{\mathbf{B}_1}, \mathbf{C}, \alpha); (\theta : \mathbf{B}^{\mathbf{B}_2}, \mathbf{C}, \alpha); \beta \overset{\mathrm{SP}*}{\Rightarrow} S/F$$

    But then

$$(\theta : (\mathbf{B}^{\mathbf{B}_1}\&\mathbf{C}) \vee (\mathbf{B}^{\mathbf{B}_2}\&\mathbf{C}), \alpha); \beta \overset{\mathrm{SP}}{\Rightarrow} (\theta : \mathbf{B}^{\mathbf{B}_1}\&\mathbf{C}, \alpha); (\theta : \mathbf{B}^{\mathbf{B}_2}\&\mathbf{C}, \alpha); \beta \overset{\mathrm{SP}}{\Rightarrow}$$

$$(\theta : \mathbf{B}^{\mathbf{B}_1}, \mathbf{C}, \alpha); (\theta : \mathbf{B}^{\mathbf{B}_2}\&\mathbf{C}, \alpha); \beta \overset{\mathrm{SP}*}{\Rightarrow} S/F$$

    because we can insert the step for splitting the second conjunction at the appropriate point if necessary. So, since $\mathbf{A}' \equiv (\mathbf{B}^{\mathbf{B}_1}\&\mathbf{C}) \vee (\mathbf{B}^{\mathbf{B}_2}\&\mathbf{C})$, the result holds.

  - The key subformula, $\mathbf{C}_1 \vee \mathbf{C}_2$, is in **C**. Thus **B** contains no disjunctions or predicate calls, and $\mathbf{A}'$ is $(\mathbf{B}\&\mathbf{C}^{\mathbf{C}_1}) \vee (\mathbf{B}\&\mathbf{C}^{\mathbf{C}_2})$. We have that

$$(\theta : \mathbf{B}, \mathbf{C}, \alpha); \beta \overset{\mathrm{SP}*}{\Rightarrow} (\theta' : \mathbf{C}, \alpha); \beta \overset{\mathrm{SP}*}{\Rightarrow} S/F$$

(because **B** contains no disjunctions, it cannot lengthen the backtrack stack). Thus, by the induction hypothesis, we have that

$$(\theta' : \mathbf{C}^{\mathbf{C}_1} \vee \mathbf{C}^{\mathbf{C}_2}, \alpha); \beta \overset{\text{SP}}{\Rightarrow} (\theta' : \mathbf{C}^{\mathbf{C}_1}, \alpha); (\theta' : \mathbf{C}^{\mathbf{C}_2}, \alpha); \beta \overset{\text{SP}*}{\Rightarrow} S/F$$

But then

$$(\theta : (\mathbf{B}\&\mathbf{C}^{\mathbf{C}_1}) \vee (\mathbf{B}\&\mathbf{C}^{\mathbf{C}_2}), \alpha); \beta \overset{\text{SP}}{\Rightarrow} (\theta : \mathbf{B}\&\mathbf{C}^{\mathbf{C}_1}, \alpha); (\theta : \mathbf{B}\&\mathbf{C}^{\mathbf{C}_2}, \alpha); \beta \overset{\text{SP}}{\Rightarrow}$$

$$(\theta : \mathbf{B}, \mathbf{C}^{\mathbf{C}_1}, \alpha); (\theta : \mathbf{B}\&\mathbf{C}^{\mathbf{C}_2}, \alpha); \beta \overset{\text{SP}*}{\Rightarrow} (\theta' : \mathbf{C}^{\mathbf{C}_1}, \alpha); (\theta : \mathbf{B}\&\mathbf{C}^{\mathbf{C}_2}, \alpha); \beta$$

$$\overset{\text{SP}*}{\Rightarrow} S/F$$

because we can insert the computation for deriving $(\theta' : \mathbf{C}^{\mathbf{C}_2}, \alpha); \beta$ from $(\theta : \mathbf{B}\&\mathbf{C}^{\mathbf{C}_2}, \alpha); \beta$ at the appropriate point if necessary. So, since $\mathbf{A}' \equiv (\mathbf{B}\&\mathbf{C}^{\mathbf{C}_1}) \vee (\mathbf{B}\&\mathbf{C}^{\mathbf{C}_2})$, the result holds.

- $\mathbf{A} \equiv \exists \mathbf{x}\mathbf{B}$. $\mathbf{A}'$ is $\exists \mathbf{x}\mathbf{B}^{\mathbf{B}_1} \vee \exists \mathbf{x}\mathbf{B}^{\mathbf{B}_2}$. We have the computation

$$(\theta : \exists \mathbf{x}\mathbf{B}, \alpha); \beta \overset{\text{SP}}{\Rightarrow} (\theta : \mathbf{B}[\mathbf{x} := \mathbf{x}'], \alpha); \beta \overset{\text{SP}*}{\Rightarrow} S/F$$

By the induction hypothesis, we have that

$$(\theta : \mathbf{B}[\mathbf{x} := \mathbf{x}']^{\mathbf{B}_1} \vee \mathbf{B}[\mathbf{x} := \mathbf{x}']^{\mathbf{B}_2}, \alpha); \beta \overset{\text{SP}}{\Rightarrow}$$

$$(\theta : \mathbf{B}[\mathbf{x} := \mathbf{x}']^{\mathbf{B}_1}, \alpha); (\theta : \mathbf{B}[\mathbf{x} := \mathbf{x}']^{\mathbf{B}_2}, \alpha); \beta \overset{\text{SP}*}{\Rightarrow} S/F$$

But then

$$(\theta : \exists \mathbf{x}\mathbf{B}^{\mathbf{B}_1} \vee \exists \mathbf{x}\mathbf{B}^{\mathbf{B}_2}, \alpha); \beta \overset{\text{SP}}{\Rightarrow} (\theta : \exists \mathbf{x}\mathbf{B}^{\mathbf{B}_1}, \alpha); (\theta : \exists \mathbf{x}\mathbf{B}^{\mathbf{B}_2}, \alpha); \beta \overset{\text{SP}}{\Rightarrow}$$

$$(\theta : \mathbf{B}[\mathbf{x} := \mathbf{x}']^{\mathbf{B}_1}, \alpha); (\theta : \exists \mathbf{x}\mathbf{B}^{\mathbf{B}_2}, \alpha); \beta \overset{\text{SP}*}{\Rightarrow} S/F$$

because we can insert the step for discharging the existential quantifier at the appropriate point if necessary (we can even use the same new variable, $\mathbf{x}'$, because if we get to that point, all other occurrences of that variable will have disappeared due to failure). So, since $\mathbf{A}' \equiv \exists \mathbf{x}\mathbf{B}^{\mathbf{B}_1} \vee \exists \mathbf{x}\mathbf{B}^{\mathbf{B}_2}$, the result holds.

This completes the proof of the forward direction of the theorem statement. We now move on to the proof of the converse.

($\leftarrow$) By induction on the depth of the key subformula (which is a disjunction) in the tree of the formula **A**.

Case depth = 0: **A** is itself a disjunction, so its disjunctive unfolding is itself. The result holds trivially.

Case depth > 0: **A** can be either a conjunction or an existential formula.

- $\mathbf{A} \equiv \mathbf{B}\&\mathbf{C}$. There are two subcases to consider.

- The key subformula, $\mathbf{B}_1 \vee \mathbf{B}_2$, is in $\mathbf{B}$. $\mathbf{A}'$ is therefore $(\mathbf{B}^{\mathbf{B}_1}\&\mathbf{C}) \vee (\mathbf{B}^{\mathbf{B}_2}\&\mathbf{C})$. We have the computation

$$(\theta : (\mathbf{B}^{\mathbf{B}_1}\&\mathbf{C}) \vee (\mathbf{B}^{\mathbf{B}_2}\&\mathbf{C}), \alpha); \beta \overset{\text{SP}}{\Rightarrow} (\theta : \mathbf{B}^{\mathbf{B}_1}\&\mathbf{C}, \alpha); (\theta : \mathbf{B}^{\mathbf{B}_2}\&\mathbf{C}, \alpha); \beta \overset{\text{SP}}{\Rightarrow}$$

$$(\theta : \mathbf{B}^{\mathbf{B}_1}, \mathbf{C}, \alpha); (\theta : \mathbf{B}^{\mathbf{B}_2}\&\mathbf{C}, \alpha); \beta \overset{\text{SP}}{\Rightarrow}^* S/F$$

But then we must have the computation

$$(\theta : \mathbf{B}^{\mathbf{B}_1} \vee \mathbf{B}^{\mathbf{B}_2}, \mathbf{C}, \alpha); \beta \overset{\text{SP}}{\Rightarrow} (\theta : \mathbf{B}^{\mathbf{B}_1}, \mathbf{C}, \alpha); (\theta : \mathbf{B}^{\mathbf{B}_2}, \mathbf{C}, \alpha); \beta \overset{\text{SP}}{\Rightarrow}^* S/F$$

because the effect of the goal stack $(\mathbf{B}^{\mathbf{B}_2}, \mathbf{C}, \alpha)$ is identical to that of $(\mathbf{B}^{\mathbf{B}_2}\&\mathbf{C}, \alpha)$ So by the induction hypothesis, we have that

$$(\theta : \mathbf{B}, \mathbf{C}, \alpha); \beta \overset{\text{SP}}{\Rightarrow}^* S/F$$

So, adding one step onto the front of the computation,

$$(\theta : \mathbf{B}\&\mathbf{C}, \alpha); \beta \overset{\text{SP}}{\Rightarrow}^* S/F$$

- The key subformula, $\mathbf{C}_1 \vee \mathbf{C}_2$, is in $\mathbf{C}$. $\mathbf{B}$ therefore contains no predicate calls or disjunctions, and $\mathbf{A}'$ is $(\mathbf{B}\&\mathbf{C}^{\mathbf{C}_1}) \vee (\mathbf{B}\&\mathbf{C}^{\mathbf{C}_2})$. We have the computation

$$(\theta : (\mathbf{B}\&\mathbf{C}^{\mathbf{C}_1}) \vee (\mathbf{B}\&\mathbf{C}^{\mathbf{C}_2}), \alpha); \beta \overset{\text{SP}}{\Rightarrow} (\theta : \mathbf{B}\&\mathbf{C}^{\mathbf{C}_1}, \alpha); (\theta : \mathbf{B}\&\mathbf{C}^{\mathbf{C}_2}, \alpha); \beta \overset{\text{SP}}{\Rightarrow}$$

$$(\theta : \mathbf{B}, \mathbf{C}^{\mathbf{C}_1}, \alpha); (\theta : \mathbf{B}\&\mathbf{C}^{\mathbf{C}_2}, \alpha); \beta \overset{\text{SP}}{\Rightarrow}^* (\theta' : \mathbf{C}^{\mathbf{C}_1}, \alpha); (\theta : \mathbf{B}\&\mathbf{C}^{\mathbf{C}_2}, \alpha); \beta$$
$$\overset{\text{SP}}{\Rightarrow}^* S/F$$

(The second-last sequence of steps does not lengthen the backtrack stack because $\mathbf{B}$ has no disjunctions or predicate calls.) But then we must have the computation

$$(\theta' : \mathbf{C}^{\mathbf{C}_1} \vee \mathbf{C}^{\mathbf{C}_2}, \alpha); \beta \overset{\text{SP}}{\Rightarrow} (\theta' : \mathbf{C}^{\mathbf{C}_1}, \alpha); (\theta' : \mathbf{C}^{\mathbf{C}_2}, \alpha); \beta \overset{\text{SP}}{\Rightarrow}^* S/F$$

because $(\theta : \mathbf{B}\&\mathbf{C}^{\mathbf{C}_2}, \alpha) \overset{\text{SP}}{\Rightarrow}^* (\theta' : \mathbf{C}^{\mathbf{C}_2}, \alpha)$. So by the induction hypothesis, we have that

$$(\theta' : \mathbf{C}, \alpha); \beta \overset{\text{SP}}{\Rightarrow}^* S/F$$

So, adding some steps onto the front of the computation,

$$(\theta : \mathbf{B}\&\mathbf{C}, \alpha); \beta \overset{\text{SP}}{\Rightarrow} (\theta : \mathbf{B}, \mathbf{C}, \alpha); \beta \overset{\text{SP}}{\Rightarrow}^* (\theta' : \mathbf{C}, \alpha); \beta \overset{\text{SP}}{\Rightarrow}^* S/F$$

- $\mathbf{A} \equiv \exists \mathbf{x}\mathbf{B}$. $\mathbf{A}'$ is $(\exists \mathbf{x}\mathbf{B}^{\mathbf{B}_1}) \vee (\exists \mathbf{x}\mathbf{B}^{\mathbf{B}_2})$. We have the computation

$$(\theta : (\exists \mathbf{x}\mathbf{B}^{\mathbf{B}_1}) \vee (\exists \mathbf{x}\mathbf{B}^{\mathbf{B}_2}), \alpha); \beta \overset{\text{SP}}{\Rightarrow} (\theta : \exists \mathbf{x}\mathbf{B}^{\mathbf{B}_1}, \alpha); (\theta : \exists \mathbf{x}\mathbf{B}^{\mathbf{B}_2}, \alpha); \beta \overset{\text{SP}}{\Rightarrow}$$

$$(\theta : \mathbf{B}^{\mathbf{B}_1}[\mathbf{x} := \mathbf{x}'], \alpha); (\theta : \exists \mathbf{x}\mathbf{B}^{\mathbf{B}_2}, \alpha); \beta \overset{\text{SP}}{\Rightarrow}^* S/F$$

But then we must have the computation

$$(\theta : \mathbf{B}^{\mathbf{B}_1}[\mathbf{x} := \mathbf{x}'] \vee \mathbf{B}^{\mathbf{B}_2}[\mathbf{x} := \mathbf{x}'], \alpha); \beta \overset{\text{SP}}{\Rightarrow}$$

$$(\theta : \mathbf{B}^{\mathbf{B}_1}[\mathbf{x} := \mathbf{x}'], \alpha); (\theta : \mathbf{B}^{\mathbf{B}_2}[\mathbf{x} := \mathbf{x}'], \alpha); \beta \overset{SP}{\Rightarrow}^* S/F$$

because $(\theta : \exists\mathbf{x}\ \mathbf{B}^{\mathbf{B}_2}, \alpha) \overset{SP}{\Rightarrow}^* (\theta : \mathbf{B}^{\mathbf{B}_2}[\mathbf{x} := \mathbf{x}'], \alpha)$. So by the induction hypothesis, we have that

$$(\theta : \mathbf{B}[\mathbf{x} := \mathbf{x}'], \alpha); \beta \overset{SP}{\Rightarrow}^* S/F$$

So, adding one step onto the front of the computation,

$$(\theta : \exists\mathbf{x}\mathbf{B}, \alpha); \beta \overset{SP}{\Rightarrow}^* S/F$$

This completes the proof of the converse direction. □

Finally, we should note that the disjunctive unfolding of a formula is classically equivalent to the formula; this follows from the distributivity of & and ∃ over ∨.

3. Axioms for Sequential Validity

With the notion of disjunctive unfolding in hand, we can now present the axioms SEQ describing validity relative to SP. Like the parallel axioms PAR, these axioms express how the signs S and F "distribute" over the goal formula connectives. In this section, I will prove these axioms sound, and in later sections I will prove the completeness results about LKE+SEQ which correspond to those of the last chapter about LKE+PAR.

The axioms are in Figure 4.3. See Appendix A for examples of the use of LKE+SEQ in deriving sequents.

As with the LKE and PAR rules, we must prove them sound. In this chapter, I will use "validity" to mean "validity with respect to SP," unless stated otherwise.

Theorem 3.1 (Validity of SEQ axioms) Each instance of the axiom schemata in SEQ is a valid sequent.

Proof : One case for each arrow direction of each axiom. We will assume that θ is a substitution which makes S closed.

$S(=)$: As in the case for PAR. For θ which makes the sequent closed, $\mathbf{s}\theta = \mathbf{t}\theta$ succeeds iff $\mathbf{s}$ and $\mathbf{t}$ are identical under θ, iff $\mathbf{s}\theta = \mathbf{t}\theta$ is valid.

$S(\&)$: As in the case for PAR. Since $\mathbf{B}$ and $\mathbf{C}$ are closed under θ, their conjunction succeeds iff each succeed independently.

$S(\vee)$, right: If $S(\mathbf{B}) \vee (F(\mathbf{B}) \& S(\mathbf{C}))$ is valid under θ, then either $\mathbf{B}\theta$ succeeds or else $\mathbf{B}\theta$ fails and $\mathbf{C}\theta$ succeeds. But since $(() : (\mathbf{B} \vee \mathbf{C})\theta) \overset{SP}{\Rightarrow} (() : \mathbf{B}\theta); (() : \mathbf{C}\theta)$, $(\mathbf{B} \vee \mathbf{C})\theta$ also succeeds.

$S(\vee)$, left: $(() : (\mathbf{B} \vee \mathbf{C})\theta \overset{SP}{\Rightarrow} (() : \mathbf{B}\theta); (() : \mathbf{C}\theta) \overset{SP}{\Rightarrow}^* (\theta' : \epsilon); \beta$. So either $(() : \mathbf{B}\theta)$ must succeed, or else $(() : \mathbf{B}\theta)$ must fail and $(() : \mathbf{C}\theta)$ succeed.

$S(\exists)$, right: Assume that θ makes the sequent closed, and that the antecedent is valid; that is, that there is a $\mathbf{t}$ such that $\mathbf{B}[\mathbf{x} := \mathbf{t}]\theta$ succeeds. Since $\mathbf{B}$ contains no predicate calls, $(\exists\mathbf{x}\ \mathbf{B})\theta$ must either succeed or fail. If it were to fail, then (by Theorem 5.2) every $\mathbf{B}[\mathbf{x} := \mathbf{s}]\theta$ would fail; so it must also succeed.

$S(\exists)$, left: By the "succeeds-one-succeeds" theorem (Theorem 5.5), if $(\exists\mathbf{x}\ \mathbf{B})\theta$ succeeds, then there must be some closed $\mathbf{t}$ such that $\mathbf{B}[\mathbf{x} := \mathbf{t}]\theta$ succeeds.

For the F rules, we must prove validity for both F^Y and F^N.

$F(=)$: As in the case for PAR. For θ which makes the sequent closed, $\mathbf{s}\theta = \mathbf{t}\theta$ fails iff $\mathbf{s}$ and $\mathbf{t}$ are non-identical closed terms, iff $\neg(\mathbf{s}\theta = \mathbf{t}\theta)$ is valid.

Success axioms:

$S(\ldots)$	left	right
=:	$S(\mathbf{s}=\mathbf{t}) \rightarrow \mathbf{s}=\mathbf{t}$	$\mathbf{s}=\mathbf{t} \rightarrow S(\mathbf{s}=\mathbf{t})$
&:	$S(\mathbf{B}\&\mathbf{C}) \rightarrow S(\mathbf{B})\&S(\mathbf{C})$	$S(\mathbf{B})\&S(\mathbf{C}) \rightarrow S(\mathbf{B}\&\mathbf{C})$
$\vee$:	$S(\mathbf{B}\vee\mathbf{C}) \rightarrow S(\mathbf{B}) \vee (F^Y(\mathbf{B})\&S(\mathbf{C}))$	$S(\mathbf{B}) \vee (F^Y(\mathbf{B})\&S(\mathbf{C})) \rightarrow S(\mathbf{B}\vee\mathbf{C})$
$\exists$:	$S(\exists\mathbf{x}\ \mathbf{B}) \rightarrow \exists\mathbf{x}\ S(\mathbf{B})$	$\exists\mathbf{x}\ S(\mathbf{B}) \rightarrow S(\exists\mathbf{x}\ \mathbf{B})$ $(*a)$

Failure axioms:

$F(\ldots)$	left	right
=:	$F(\mathbf{s}=\mathbf{t}) \rightarrow \neg\mathbf{s}=\mathbf{t}$	$\neg\mathbf{s}=\mathbf{t} \rightarrow F(\mathbf{s}=\mathbf{t})$
&:	$F(\mathbf{B}\&\mathbf{C}) \rightarrow F(\mathbf{B}) \vee (S(\mathbf{B})\&F(\mathbf{C}))$	(1) $F(\mathbf{B}) \rightarrow F(\mathbf{B}\&\mathbf{C})$ (2) $F(\mathbf{B}) \vee F(\mathbf{C}) \rightarrow F(\mathbf{B}\&\mathbf{C})$ $(*a)$
$\vee$:	$F(\mathbf{B}\vee\mathbf{C}) \rightarrow F(\mathbf{B})\&F(\mathbf{C})$	$F(\mathbf{B})\&F(\mathbf{C}) \rightarrow F(\mathbf{B}\vee\mathbf{C})$
$\exists$:	$F(\exists\mathbf{x}\ \mathbf{B}) \rightarrow \forall\mathbf{x}\ F(\mathbf{B})$	$\forall\mathbf{x}\ F^N(\mathbf{B}) \rightarrow F(\exists\mathbf{x}\ \mathbf{B})$

Miscellaneous axioms:

	left	right
F^N/F^Y:		$F^N(\mathbf{A}) \rightarrow F^Y(\mathbf{A})$
Unf:	$\sigma(\mathbf{A}) \rightarrow \sigma(\mathbf{A}')$ $(*b)$	$\sigma(\mathbf{A}') \rightarrow \sigma(\mathbf{A})$ $(*b)$
Disj:	$\sigma(\mathbf{A}) \rightarrow \sigma(\mathbf{A}')$ $(*c)$	$\sigma(\mathbf{A}') \rightarrow \sigma(\mathbf{A})$ $(*c)$
$F^N(\mathbf{P})$:	$F^N(\mathbf{P}(\mathbf{t}_1,\ldots,\mathbf{t}_n)) \rightarrow$	

Side-conditions:
$(*a)$ **B** contains no predicate calls
$(*b)$ $\mathbf{A}'$ is a predicate unfolding of **A**, and σ is either S or F^Y
$(*c)$ $\mathbf{A}'$ is the disjunctive unfolding of **A**, and σ is either S or F^Y

Figure 4.3. SEQ axioms characterising sequential connectives. F means either F^Y or F^N, its use being consistent throughout each axiom.

$F(\&)$, left: $(() : (\mathbf{B}\&\mathbf{C})\theta \stackrel{SP}{\Rightarrow} (() : \mathbf{B}\theta, \mathbf{C}\theta) \stackrel{SP*}{\Rightarrow} \epsilon$. So either $\mathbf{B}\theta$ fails without even reaching $\mathbf{C}\theta$, or else $\mathbf{B}\theta$ succeeds but $\mathbf{C}\theta$ fails. If $(\mathbf{B}\&\mathbf{C})\theta$ fails flatly, then so do the subsidiary computations. (This is clearly not all the information we can extract from the fact that $(\mathbf{B}\&\mathbf{C})\theta$ fails; see the discussion on the inversion principle at the end of this chapter.)

$F(\&)$, right, 1: If $(() : \mathbf{B}\theta) \stackrel{SP*}{\Rightarrow} \epsilon$, we can graft the formula $\mathbf{C}\theta$ onto every closure in that computation to get a failing computation of $(() : \mathbf{B}\theta, \mathbf{C}\theta)$. But $(() : (\mathbf{B}\&\mathbf{C})\theta) \stackrel{SP}{\Rightarrow} (() : \mathbf{B}\theta, \mathbf{C}\theta)$, so $(\mathbf{B}\&\mathbf{C})\theta$ fails too. If $\mathbf{B}\theta$ fails flatly, then so does the new computation.

$F(\&)$, right, 2: If the antecedent is valid under θ, then either $\mathbf{B}\theta$ fails or $\mathbf{C}\theta$ fails. If $\mathbf{B}\theta$ fails, then $(() : \mathbf{B}\theta, \mathbf{C}\theta)$ must fail too; so $(\mathbf{B}\&\mathbf{C})\theta$ fails. If $\mathbf{B}\theta$ does not fail, then (since it contains no predicate calls) it must succeed, and $\mathbf{C}\theta$ must fail for the antecedent to be valid; so again $(() : \mathbf{B}\theta, \mathbf{C}\theta)$ must fail.

$F(\vee)$: As in the case for PAR. $(() : \mathbf{B}\theta); (() : \mathbf{C}\theta)$ fails iff both closures fail independently; and fails flatly iff both closures fail flatly.

$F(\exists)$, left: As in the case for PAR. By the "fails-all-fail" theorem (Theorem 5.2), if $(\exists\mathbf{x}\ \mathbf{B})\theta$ fails, then every instance of $\mathbf{B}\theta$ fails, and the restriction to flat failure holds as well.

$F(\exists)$, right: As in the case for PAR. If every instance of $\mathbf{B}\theta$ fails flatly, we can (by the techniques of this case in the PAR validity proof) prove that $(\exists\mathbf{x}\ \mathbf{B})\theta$ fails.

F^N/F^Y: If $\mathbf{A}$ fails flatly, then it clearly fails.

Disj, Unf: by Theorems 3.2 and 2.2.

$F^N(\mathbf{P})$: Clearly, no predicate call can fail without performing at least one Defined Predicate step. □

The reason for the restriction on the $F(\&)$, right, 2 rule should be clear from the example given in the last section. The corresponding example justifying the restriction on the $S(\exists)$, right rule is the following query:

$$\exists x((x = 0\&Loop()) \vee x = 1)$$

Obviously, the query $(1 = 0\&Loop()) \vee 1 = 1$ succeeds, so the assertion $\exists x S((x = 0\&Loop()) \vee x = 1)$ is valid; but the query itself does not succeed. As in the case for $F(\&)$, though, the disjunctive unfolding of the query (in this case $\exists x(x = 0\&Loop()) \vee \exists x(x = 1)$) behaves properly.

Finally, we have the comprehensive Soundness result for LKE+SEQ.

Theorem 3.2 (Soundness of LKE+SEQ) Every sequent derivable in LKE+SEQ is valid.

Proof : By induction on the structure of the derivation. Cases are from the Validity theorems for LKE and SEQ. □

4. Completeness: Closed Assertions

We have the same kinds of completeness results for LKE+SEQ with respect to sequential validity as we did for LKE+PAR with respect to parallel validity. Many of the theorems are proved in very similar ways as those in the last chapter; I will omit these details, and concentrate on the cases in the proofs which are different from those for PAR.

The completeness theorem suggests a possible (inefficient) strategy for deciding sequents consisting of signed formulae. Informally, we decompose the formulae in the sequent using the appropriate connective axioms from SEQ. If we come to formulae which do not meet the side-conditions on the appropriate rules, we apply a finite number of predicate unfolding steps, followed possibly by a disjunctive unfolding step. We then proceed as before. This strategy will always work for valid sequents, because each step decreases the number of steps in the computation of the sequent.

Theorem 4.1 (Closed Completeness, stage 1) All valid sequents $\mathcal{S}$ which have only equalities in the antecedent, and only equalities and F^N formulae in the consequent, are derivable in LKE+SEQ.

Proof : As in the proof of the corresponding theorem for PAR, by induction on the number of connectives and equality formulae within F^N signs. If this number is 0, then by the Completeness Theorem for Equality, Theorem 4.3, the result holds.

Otherwise, let $\mathcal{S}$ be $\Gamma \rightarrow \Delta, F^N(\mathbf{D}_1), \ldots, F^N(\mathbf{D}_m)$, where the Δ formulae are all equalities. Cases are on $\mathbf{D}_1$. We will derive sequents which must also be valid, and which have fewer connectives and equality formulae within F^N signs.

$\mathbf{D}_1 \equiv (\mathbf{s} = \mathbf{t})$: as in the proof for PAR.

$\mathbf{D}_1 \equiv \mathbf{B}\&\mathbf{C}$: Assume that $\mathcal{S}$ is valid. There are three subcases. If **B** contains no predicate calls, then under every substitution, **B** must either succeed or fail. Consider the sequent $\mathcal{S}'$ formed by replacing $F^N(\mathbf{B}\&\mathbf{C})$ by $F^N(\mathbf{B}), F^N(\mathbf{C})$. If $\mathcal{S}'$ were invalid, then there would be a substitution under which neither $F^N(\mathbf{B}), F^N(\mathbf{C})$ nor any of the other signed formulae in $\mathcal{S}$ would be valid; but if that were true, $\mathbf{B}\theta$ would succeed (since it cannot diverge or fail non-flatly), and $\mathbf{C}\theta$ would not fail flatly, making $F^N(\mathbf{B}\&\mathbf{C})\theta$ invalid, and thus making $\mathcal{S}$ invalid. So $\mathcal{S}'$ must be valid; by the induction hypothesis, it is derivable; and $\mathcal{S}$ can be derived from it by $\vee$,r and Cut with $F(\&)$,right,2 from SEQ.

If **B** contains predicate calls and its key subformula is a predicate call, then let $\mathcal{S}'$ be $\mathcal{S}$ with $F^N(\mathbf{B}\&\mathbf{C})$ replaced by $F^N(\mathbf{B})$. If $F^N(\mathbf{B})$ were invalid under θ, then $\mathbf{B}\theta$ must either succeed (in which case it *must* make a predicate call, since its key subformula must eventually get to the top of the goal stack), fail non-flatly (in which case $(\mathbf{B}\&\mathbf{C})\theta$ also fails non-flatly) or diverge (in which case $(\mathbf{B}\&\mathbf{C})\theta$ also diverges); so $F^N(\mathbf{B}\&\mathbf{C})$ would also be invalid under θ. So $\mathcal{S}'$ is valid; by the induction hypothesis, it is derivable; and $\mathcal{S}$ can be derived from it by Cut with $F(\&)$,right,1 from SEQ.

Finally, if **B** contains predicate calls and its key subformula is a disjunction $\mathbf{B}_1 \vee \mathbf{B}_2$, then the disjunctive unfolding of $\mathbf{B}\&\mathbf{C}$ must be $(\mathbf{B}^{\mathbf{B}_1}\&\mathbf{C}) \vee (\mathbf{B}^{\mathbf{B}_2}\&\mathbf{C})$. Let $\mathcal{S}_1$ be $\mathcal{S}$ with $F^N(\mathbf{B}\&\mathbf{C})$ replaced by $F^N(\mathbf{B}^{\mathbf{B}_1}\&\mathbf{C})$, and let $\mathcal{S}_2$ be $\mathcal{S}$ with $F^N(\mathbf{B}\&\mathbf{C})$ replaced by $F^N(\mathbf{B}^{\mathbf{B}_2}\&\mathbf{C})$. Then $\mathcal{S}_1$ must be valid, because if there were no flatly failing computation for $\mathbf{B}^{\mathbf{B}_2}\&\mathbf{C}$ then there could be no flatly failing computation for $\mathbf{B}\&\mathbf{C}$, since the start of the computation of $\mathbf{B}\&\mathbf{C}$ is essentially the same except for the $\vee$ step. Similarly, $\mathcal{S}_2$ must be valid because otherwise the tail of the computation of $\mathbf{B}\&\mathbf{C}$ could not result in flat failure. But since both $\mathcal{S}_1$ and $\mathcal{S}_2$ have one fewer connective (the $\vee$ is missing), by the induction hypothesis they must be both derivable. $\mathcal{S}$ is derivable from $\mathcal{S}_1$ and $\mathcal{S}_2$ by an application of $\&, r$, an application of Cut with $F(\vee)$, right, and an application of Cut with Disj, right from SEQ.

$\mathbf{D}_1 \equiv \mathbf{B} \vee \mathbf{C}$: If $\mathbf{B} \vee \mathbf{C}$ fails flatly under θ, then both **B** and **C** must fail flatly under θ. So both $\mathcal{S}$ with $\mathbf{B} \vee \mathbf{C}$ replaced by **B** and $\mathcal{S}$ with $\mathbf{B} \vee \mathbf{C}$ replaced by **C** must be valid; by the induction hypothesis, they are both derivable; and $\mathcal{S}$ can be derived from them by using the $\&, r$ rule and Cut with $F(\vee)$, right from SEQ.

$\mathbf{D}_1 \equiv \exists \mathbf{x}\ \mathbf{B}$: As in the proof for PAR: we can use $\forall$,r and $F(\exists)$,right from SEQ to derive $\mathcal{S}$ from a valid sequent of lower measure. □

The results in the last chapter about predicate unfoldings and about failing computations both extend to computations in SP. They are not simple consequences of those results, but the proofs are similar.

Lemma 4.2 If a backtrack stack β fails, then some predicate unfolding of β can fail flatly.

Proof : As in the last chapter. □

Theorem 4.3 (Closed Completeness, stage 2a) All valid sequents $\mathcal{S}$ of the form $[\rightarrow F^Y(\mathbf{A})]$, where **A** is a closed formula, are derivable in LKE+SEQ.

Proof : As in the last chapter. We can unfold **A** until it fails flatly. □

Theorem 4.4 (Closed Completeness, stage 2b) All valid sequents $\mathcal{S}$ of the form $[\rightarrow S(\mathbf{A})]$, where $\mathbf{A}$ is a closed formula, are derivable in LKE+SEQ.

Proof : By the definition of validity, $(() : \mathbf{A})$ must succeed. We can proceed by induction on the length of this computation. Cases are on the form of $\mathbf{A}$.

$\mathbf{A} \equiv (\mathbf{s} = \mathbf{t})$: As in the theorem for PAR. $\mathbf{s}$ and $\mathbf{t}$ are closed, and so must be identical for them to unify. We can therefore derive $\mathcal{S}$ from an Eq axiom and an application of Cut with the $S(=)$, right axiom of SEQ.

$\mathbf{A} \equiv \mathbf{B}\&\mathbf{C}$: As in the theorem for PAR. $\mathbf{B}$ and $\mathbf{C}$ must succeed independently, one after another, each with a shorter computation than $\mathbf{B}\&\mathbf{C}$. $\mathcal{S}$ must therefore be derivable from $[\rightarrow S(\mathbf{B})]$ and $[\rightarrow S(\mathbf{C})]$ by &,r and Cut with $S(\&)$,right of SEQ.

$\mathbf{A} \equiv \mathbf{B} \vee \mathbf{C}$: The first step of the computation is $(() : \mathbf{B} \vee \mathbf{C}) \stackrel{SP}{\Rightarrow} (() : \mathbf{B}); (() : \mathbf{C})$. Clearly either $\mathbf{B}$ succeeds (in which case $\mathcal{S}$ is derivable from $[\rightarrow S(\mathbf{B})]$ by Thin,r and $\vee$,r and Cut with $S(\vee)$, right from SEQ), or else $\mathbf{B}$ fails and $\mathbf{C}$ succeeds (in which case $\mathcal{S}$ is derivable from $[\rightarrow F(\mathbf{B})]$ and $[\rightarrow S(\mathbf{C})]$ by $\&, r$, Thin,r, and $\vee$,r and Cut with $S(\vee)$,r from SEQ).

$\mathbf{A} \equiv \exists \mathbf{x}\ \mathbf{B}$: There are three subcases. First, let $\mathbf{B}$ have no predicate calls. By the "succeeds-one-succeeds" theorem (Theorem 5.5), there must be a $\mathbf{t}$ such that $\mathbf{B}[\mathbf{x} := \mathbf{t}]$ succeeds. This successful computation is the same length or shorter than the computation of $\mathbf{B}$, namely one step shorter than the computation of $\exists \mathbf{x}\ \mathbf{B}$; so $[\rightarrow S(\mathbf{B}[\mathbf{x} := \mathbf{t}])]$ is derivable, and $\mathcal{S}$ can be derived from it by $\exists$,r and Cut with $S(\exists)$,r from SEQ.

If $\mathbf{B}$ contains predicate calls, and its key subformula is a predicate call, then that key subformula must come to the top of the goal stack during the course of the successful computation. The predicate 1-expansion $\mathbf{A}'$ of $\mathbf{A}$ in which the key subformula is expanded therefore must take one fewer step than that of $\mathbf{A}$. $\mathcal{S}$ is therefore derivable from $[\rightarrow S(\mathbf{A}')]$ by Cut with Unf,r of SEQ.

Finally, if $\mathbf{B}$ contains predicate calls but its key subformula is a disjunction $\mathbf{B}_1 \vee \mathbf{B}_2$, then by Theorem 2.2, $\mathbf{A}$'s disjunctive unfolding $\mathbf{A}^{\mathbf{B}_1} \vee \mathbf{A}^{\mathbf{B}_2}$ must succeed. We can follow similar reasoning to the $\vee$ case, above, to show that either $[\rightarrow S(\mathbf{A}^{\mathbf{B}_1})]$ is valid, or both $[\rightarrow F(\mathbf{A}^{\mathbf{B}_1})]$ and $[\rightarrow S(\mathbf{A}^{\mathbf{B}_2})]$ are valid; but all of these will correspond to shorter computations than $\mathbf{A}$, and so are derivable; so $\mathcal{S}$ is derivable by using &,r and $\vee$,r from LKE, Cut with $S(\vee)$, right from SEQ, and Cut with Disj,r of SEQ.

$\mathbf{A} \equiv \mathbf{P}(\mathbf{t}_1, \ldots, \mathbf{t}_n)$: As in the theorem for PAR; as in the last case, we can use Cut with Unf, right from SEQ to get a sequent which is valid and takes fewer computation steps, and which thus is derivable. □

The rest of the stages are as in the last chapter.

Theorem 4.5 (Closed Completeness, stage 3) All valid sequents $\mathcal{S}$ which have only equalities in the antecedent, and only equalities and signed formulae in the consequent, and where no free variable appears in any S or F^Y assertion, are derivable in LKE+SEQ.

Proof : As in the last chapter. We can either thin out all but a valid S or F^Y formula, or thin out all the S and F^Y formulae, and by stages 1, 2a, and 2b, we will be able to derive the resulting sequent. □

Theorem 4.6 (Closed Completeness, stage 4) All valid sequents $\mathcal{S}$ in which no free variable appears in an S or F^Y subassertion, and no signed formula appears in a negative context, are derivable in LKE+SEQ.

Proof : As in the last chapter: by induction on the total number of connectives outside signed formulae. □

Finally, we have the important results about the characterisation of successful and failing queries corresponding to that in the last chapter.

Theorem 4.7 (Characterisation of SP) A goal formula **A** succeeds in SP iff the sequent $[\rightarrow S(\exists[\mathbf{A}])]$ is derivable in LKE+SEQ; it fails in SP iff the sequent $[\rightarrow F^Y(\exists[\mathbf{A}])]$ is derivable in LKE+SEQ.

Proof : As in the last chapter: from the Soundness and Completeness theorems. □

So just as LKE+PAR characterised the two outer circles from the Venn diagram (Figure 2.6), LKE+SEQ has succeeded in characterising the two innermost circles from that diagram. A query **A** is in the innermost failure set iff $[\rightarrow F(\exists[\mathbf{A}])]$ is derivable; a query **A** is in the innermost success set iff $[\rightarrow S(\exists[\mathbf{A}])]$ is derivable. Because of the completeness property of SOS/sa, we have also characterised the queries which fail in SOS/sa.

5. Completeness: Predicate-Free Assertions

The results about predicate-free assertions in PAR extend to SEQ in a simpler way than did the results about closed assertions. This is because predicate-free backtrack stacks either succeed or fail, and do not diverge; so SP is actually complete with respect to SOS for such backtrack stacks.

Theorem 5.1 (Flat Completeness, stage 1) All valid sequents $\mathcal{S}$ containing no signed formulae are derivable in LKE.

Proof : If $\mathcal{S}$ is valid with respect to SP, then it is also valid with respect to SOS; thus, by the Flat Completeness, stage 1 theorem in the last chapter, it is derivable. □

Theorem 5.2 (Flat Completeness, stage 2) All valid sequents $\mathcal{S}$ containing no predicate calls are derivable in LKE+SEQ.

Proof : As in the last chapter. The more restrictive side-conditions do not apply, since none of the signed formulae contain predicate calls; the different forms of some of the rules do not seriously affect the proof. □

The results about hierarchical programs extend to SEQ as well.

Theorem 5.3 If Π is hierarchical, then all valid sequents $\mathcal{S}$ are derivable in LKE+SEQ.

Proof : As in the last chapter: we can unfold predicate calls until none are left in the sequent. □

6. Success for SOS/so

The last circle on the Venn diagram in Figure 2.6 left to be characterised is the middle success set – the set of queries succeeding in SOS/so. The set of *failing* queries for SOS/so is exactly that for SOS, so we have no need of further characterising that set; and for the successful queries, it turns out that a proof system essentially consisting of the success axioms from SEQ and the failure axioms from PAR will serve to characterise this class.

Success axioms:

$S(\ldots)$	left	right
$=$:	$S(\mathbf{s}=\mathbf{t}) \rightarrow \mathbf{s}=\mathbf{t}$	$\mathbf{s}=\mathbf{t} \rightarrow S(\mathbf{s}=\mathbf{t})$
&:	$S(\mathbf{B}\&\mathbf{C}) \rightarrow S(\mathbf{B})\&S(\mathbf{C})$	$S(\mathbf{B})\&S(\mathbf{C}) \rightarrow S(\mathbf{B}\&\mathbf{C})$
$\vee$:	$S(\mathbf{B} \vee \mathbf{C}) \rightarrow S(\mathbf{B}) \vee (F^Y(\mathbf{B})\&S(\mathbf{C}))$ $S(\mathbf{B}) \vee (F^Y(\mathbf{B})\&S(\mathbf{C})) \rightarrow S(\mathbf{B} \vee \mathbf{C})$	
$\exists$:	$S(\exists \mathbf{x}\ \mathbf{B}) \rightarrow \exists \mathbf{x}\ S(\mathbf{B})$	$\exists \mathbf{x}\ S(\mathbf{B}) \rightarrow S(\exists \mathbf{x}\ \mathbf{B})$ $(*a)$

Failure axioms:

$F(\ldots)$	left	right
$=$:	$F(\mathbf{s}=\mathbf{t}) \rightarrow \neg\mathbf{s}=\mathbf{t}$	$\neg\mathbf{s}=\mathbf{t} \rightarrow F(\mathbf{s}=\mathbf{t})$
&:	$F(\mathbf{B}\&\mathbf{C}) \rightarrow F(\mathbf{B}) \vee F(\mathbf{C})$	$F(\mathbf{B}) \vee F(\mathbf{C}) \rightarrow F(\mathbf{B}\&\mathbf{C})$
$\vee$:	$F(\mathbf{B} \vee \mathbf{C}) \rightarrow F(\mathbf{B})\&F(\mathbf{C})$	$F(\mathbf{B})\&F(\mathbf{C}) \rightarrow F(\mathbf{B} \vee \mathbf{C})$
$\exists$:	$F(\exists \mathbf{x}\ \mathbf{B}) \rightarrow \forall \mathbf{x}\ F(\mathbf{B})$	$\forall \mathbf{x}\ F^N(\mathbf{B}) \rightarrow F(\exists \mathbf{x}\ \mathbf{B})$

Miscellaneous axioms:

	left	right
F^N/F^Y:		$F^N(\mathbf{A}) \rightarrow F^Y(\mathbf{A})$
Unf:	$\sigma(\mathbf{A}) \rightarrow \sigma(\mathbf{A}')$ $(*b)$	$\sigma(\mathbf{A}') \rightarrow \sigma(\mathbf{A})$ $(*b)$
Disj:	$\sigma(\mathbf{A}) \rightarrow \sigma(\mathbf{A}')$ $(*c)$	$\sigma(\mathbf{A}') \rightarrow \sigma(\mathbf{A})$ $(*c)$
$F^N(\mathbf{P})$:	$F^N(\mathbf{P}(\mathbf{t}_1, \ldots, \mathbf{t}_n)) \rightarrow$	

Side-conditions:
$(*a)$ **B** contains no predicate calls
$(*b)$ $\mathbf{A}'$ is a predicate unfolding of **A**, and σ is either S or F^Y
$(*c)$ $\mathbf{A}'$ is the disjunctive unfolding of **A**, and σ is either S or F^Y

Figure 4.4. PASO axioms characterising SOS/so. F means either F^Y or F^N, its use being consistent throughout each axiom.

As we saw in Chapter 2, the set of successful queries for SOS/so is smaller than the set of successful queries for SOS because the sequential "or" misses some solutions; but it is also bigger than the set of successful queries for SP, because the parallel "and" causes more queries to fail, and this has the knock-on effect of allowing some more queries to succeed.

This effect of the expansion of the set of failing queries is illustrated well in the set of axioms PASO ("Parallel And, Sequential Or"; Fig. 4.4). The Success and Miscellaneous axioms of PASO are exactly those from SEQ, but the Failure axioms are exactly those from PAR. We are therefore able to prove more things to be failing than in SEQ (for example, *Loop*()&*false*); and because the $S(\vee)$ axioms depend on failure, we are therefore able to prove more things successful than in SEQ (for example, (*Loop*()&*false*) $\vee$ *true*, the example from Chapter 2). See the Appendix for a derivation of the success of this query in LKE+PASO.

We must prove these axioms to be sound, and prove the equivalents of the Closed Completeness results, of course. However, many of the results we need to prove follow directly from those in this chapter and the previous one, and others have very similar proofs. I will briefly outline the results, noting only where they differ from those for PAR and SEQ.

Theorem 6.1 (SOS/so Equivalence of Disjunctive Unfoldings) If $\mathbf{A} \stackrel{\text{Disj}}{\Rightarrow} \mathbf{A}'$, then $(\theta : \mathbf{A}, \alpha); \beta$ succeeds (fails) in SOS/so iff $(\theta : \mathbf{A}', \alpha); \beta$ succeeds (fails) in SOS/so.

Proof : This is much the same as in the case for SEQ; I will sketch it here. The proof is by induction on the depth of the key subformula, a disjunction, in $\mathbf{A}$.

Case depth = 0: $\mathbf{A}$ is itself a disjunction, so its disjunctive unfolding is itself. The result holds trivially.

Case depth > 0: $\mathbf{A}$ can be either a conjunction or an existential formula.

- $\mathbf{A} \equiv \mathbf{B}\&\mathbf{C}$, and the key subformula, $\mathbf{B}_1 \vee \mathbf{B}_2$, is in $\mathbf{B}$. If one of the following goal stacks succeeds (resp. fails) in SOS/so, all the rest succeed (resp. fail) in SOS/so:

$$(\theta : \mathbf{B}\&\mathbf{C}, \alpha)$$

$$(\theta : \mathbf{B}, \mathbf{C}, \alpha)$$
$$(\theta : \mathbf{B}^{\mathbf{B}_1} \vee \mathbf{B}^{\mathbf{B}_2}, \mathbf{C}, \alpha) \quad *$$
$$(\theta : \mathbf{B}^{\mathbf{B}_1}, \mathbf{C}, \alpha); (\theta : \mathbf{B}^{\mathbf{B}_2}, \mathbf{C}, \alpha)$$
$$(\theta : \mathbf{B}^{\mathbf{B}_1}\&\mathbf{C}, \alpha); (\theta : \mathbf{B}^{\mathbf{B}_2}\&\mathbf{C}, \alpha)$$
$$(\theta : (\mathbf{B}^{\mathbf{B}_1}\&\mathbf{C}) \vee (\mathbf{B}^{\mathbf{B}_2}\&\mathbf{C}), \alpha)$$

  where the step $*$ is from the induction hypothesis. Since $\mathbf{A}' \equiv (\mathbf{B}^{\mathbf{B}_1}\&\mathbf{C}) \vee (\mathbf{B}^{\mathbf{B}_2}\&\mathbf{C})$, the result holds.

- $\mathbf{A} \equiv \mathbf{B}\&\mathbf{C}$, and the key subformula, $\mathbf{C}_1 \vee \mathbf{C}_2$, is in $\mathbf{C}$. If one of the following goal stacks succeeds (resp. fails) in SOS/so, all the rest succeed (resp. fail) in SOS/so:

$$(\theta : \mathbf{B}\&\mathbf{C}, \alpha)$$

$$(\theta : \mathbf{B}, \mathbf{C}, \alpha)$$
$$(\theta : \mathbf{B}, \mathbf{C}^{\mathbf{C}_1} \vee \mathbf{C}^{\mathbf{C}_2}, \alpha) \quad *$$
$$(\theta : \mathbf{B}, \mathbf{C}^{\mathbf{C}_1}, \alpha); (\theta : \mathbf{B}, \mathbf{C}^{\mathbf{C}_2}, \alpha)$$
$$(\theta : \mathbf{B}\&\mathbf{C}^{\mathbf{C}_1}, \alpha); (\theta : \mathbf{B}\&\mathbf{C}^{\mathbf{C}_2}, \alpha)$$
$$(\theta : (\mathbf{B}\&\mathbf{C}^{\mathbf{C}_1}) \vee (\mathbf{B}\&\mathbf{C}^{\mathbf{C}_2}), \alpha)$$

  where the step $*$ is from the induction hypothesis. Since $\mathbf{A}' \equiv (\mathbf{B}\&\mathbf{C}^{\mathbf{C}_1}) \vee (\mathbf{B}\&\mathbf{C}^{\mathbf{C}_2})$, the result holds.

- $\mathbf{A} \equiv \exists \mathbf{x}\ \mathbf{B}$. If one of the following goal stacks succeeds (resp. fails) in SOS/so, all the rest succeed (resp. fail) in SOS/so:

$$(\theta : \exists \mathbf{x}\ \mathbf{B}, \alpha)$$

$$(\theta : \mathbf{B}[\mathbf{x} := \mathbf{x}'], \alpha)$$
$$(\theta : \mathbf{B}^{\mathbf{B}_1}[\mathbf{x} := \mathbf{x}'] \vee \mathbf{B}^{\mathbf{B}_2}[\mathbf{x} := \mathbf{x}'], \alpha) \quad *$$
$$(\theta : \mathbf{B}^{\mathbf{B}_1}[\mathbf{x} := \mathbf{x}'], \alpha); (\theta : \mathbf{B}^{\mathbf{B}_2}[\mathbf{x} := \mathbf{x}'], \alpha)$$

$$(\theta : \mathbf{B}^{\mathbf{B}_1}[\mathbf{x} := \mathbf{x}'], \alpha); (\theta : \mathbf{B}^{\mathbf{B}_2}[\mathbf{x} := \mathbf{x}''], \alpha)$$
$$(\theta : \exists \mathbf{x}\ \mathbf{B}^{\mathbf{B}_1}, \alpha); (\theta : \mathbf{B}^{\mathbf{B}_2}[\mathbf{x} := \mathbf{x}''], \alpha)$$
$$(\theta : \exists \mathbf{x}\ \mathbf{B}^{\mathbf{B}_1}, \alpha); (\theta : \exists \mathbf{x}\ \mathbf{B}^{\mathbf{B}_2}, \alpha)$$
$$(\theta : \exists \mathbf{x}\ \mathbf{B}^{\mathbf{B}_1} \vee \exists \mathbf{x}\ \mathbf{B}^{\mathbf{B}_2}, \alpha)$$

where the step $*$ is from the induction hypothesis. Since $\mathbf{A}' \equiv \exists \mathbf{x}\ \mathbf{B}^{\mathbf{B}_1} \vee \exists \mathbf{x}\ \mathbf{B}^{\mathbf{B}_2}$, the result holds.

□

Theorem 6.2 (Validity of PASO Axioms) Each instance of the axiom schemata in PASO is valid with respect to SOS/so.

Proof : The Failure group is identical to the one found in PAR. The only signed formulae they contain are F-signed formulae, which are valid wrt SOS/so iff they are valid wrt SOS (by the completeness results in Chapter 2); so, since we have proven them valid wrt SOS in the validity proof for PAR, they are also valid wrt SOS/so. The same holds for the Miscellaneous axioms that have only F-signed formulae.

The proofs for the other axioms are much as in the case for SEQ. The "and" is now parallel, but the logic remains the same: if $(\mathbf{B}\theta \& \mathbf{C}\theta)$ is closed, then it succeeds iff both $\mathbf{B}\theta$ and $\mathbf{C}\theta$ succeed independently. The validity of the Disj axioms follows from the operational equivalence of disjunctive unfolding for SOS/so (Theorem 6.1). All other axioms follow the pattern of SEQ. □

In the completeness results, the only stage that needs to be re-proved is Closed Completeness, stage 2b:

Theorem 6.3 (Closed Completeness, stage 2b) All sequents $\mathcal{S}$ valid wrt SOS/so and of the form $[\rightarrow S(\mathbf{A})]$, where $\mathbf{A}$ is a closed formula, are derivable in LKE+PASO.

Proof: Almost identical to the case for SEQ. The only case that is significantly different is $S(\exists)$. There, we must prove that if $\exists \mathbf{x}\ \mathbf{B}$ is closed and succeeds, then $[\rightarrow S(\exists \mathbf{x}\ \mathbf{B})]$ is derivable, given the induction hypothesis. There are three subcases.

In the case that $\mathbf{B}$ contains no predicate calls, we can apply the $S(\exists)$, right axiom straightforwardly, because the "succeeds-one-succeeds" theorem (Theorem 5.5) guarantees that there is a witness.

If $\mathbf{B}$ contains predicate calls and its key subformula is a predicate call, then the proof is not quite so straightforward as in the case for SEQ. Because we have parallel "and", the closure may be split up into several due to some disjunction to the right of the key subformula; for example,

$$(\theta_1 : \ldots \mathbf{P}(\ldots), \ldots, \mathbf{B} \vee \mathbf{C}) \stackrel{\mathrm{SOS/so}}{\Rightarrow} (\theta_1 : \ldots \mathbf{P}(\ldots), \ldots, \mathbf{B}); (\theta_1 : \ldots \mathbf{P}(\ldots), \ldots, \mathbf{C})$$

However, it is still the case that since the query succeeds, the key subformula must eventually be computed *in at least one* of the resultant closures. Thus, the predicate 1-unfolding of $\mathbf{B}$ in which the key subformula is unfolded must have an SOS/so-computation of fewer steps. The induction hypothesis applies, and we can therefore derive $[\rightarrow S(\exists \mathbf{x}\ \mathbf{B})]$ from the derivable $[\rightarrow S(\exists \mathbf{x}\ \mathbf{B}')]$, where $\mathbf{B}'$ is this predicate 1-unfolding of $\mathbf{B}$.

If **B** contains predicate calls and its key subformula is a disjunction, then (by the operational equivalence of disjunctive unfoldings, Theorem 6.1) the disjunctive unfolding of $\exists\mathbf{x}\ \mathbf{B}$, $\exists\mathbf{x}\ \mathbf{B}^{\mathbf{B}_1} \vee \exists\mathbf{x}\ \mathbf{B}^{\mathbf{B}_2}$, must also succeed. But then, as in the case for SEQ, we can use the $S(\vee)$, right axiom to derive $[\rightarrow S(\exists\mathbf{x}\ \mathbf{B}^{\mathbf{B}_1} \vee \exists\mathbf{x}\ \mathbf{B}^{\mathbf{B}_2})]$ from either $[\rightarrow S(\exists\mathbf{x}\ \mathbf{B}^{\mathbf{B}_1})]$ or from $[\rightarrow F(\exists\mathbf{x}\ \mathbf{B}^{\mathbf{B}_1})]$ and $[\rightarrow S(\exists\mathbf{x}\ \mathbf{B}^{\mathbf{B}_2})]$. □

Stages 1 and 2a of Closed Completeness are about failing formulae, and thus follow from the corresponding stages from PAR. Stages 3 and 4 follow the proofs for PAR and SEQ exactly. We therefore have the following important characterisation result corresponding to those for PAR and SEQ:

Theorem 6.4 (Characterisation of SOS/so) A goal formula **A** succeeds in SOS/so iff the sequent $[\rightarrow S(\exists[\mathbf{A}])]$ is derivable in LKE+PASO; it fails in SOS/so iff the sequent $[\rightarrow F^Y(\exists[\mathbf{A}])]$ is derivable in LKE+PASO.

Proof : As in the case for PAR and SEQ: from the Soundness and Completeness theorems. □

Finally, as with SEQ, the Flat Completeness results go through unchanged because all sequents containing no predicate calls have the property that they are either valid with respect to all variants of SOS, or invalid with respect to all variants.

These soundness and completeness results complete our logical characterisation of the queries succeeding and failing in the various control disciplines. The characterisation is especially pleasing because the three characterising proof systems share the common rules LKE, and because the PASO rules integrate the PAR and SEQ rules in a simple and intuitively clear way.

7. Discussion

Some comments from the Discussion section of Chapter 3 apply to the material in this chapter as well. These include the discussion of more practical failure rules. Here, I concentrate on issues surrounding SEQ in particular, and its correspondence to SP; these comments apply equally to PASO and its correspondence to SOS/so.

7.1. SEQ as a Characterisation of SP

Our goal, in this chapter, has been to find a logical characterisation of sequential logic programming. Is LKE+SEQ such a characterisation? By Theorem 4.7, it is a characterisation, but is it logical? The answer to this question hinges on whether we consider the non-compositional elements of SEQ (the predicate and disjunctive unfolding rules) to be "logical" enough.

Shoenfield [69] has discussed the related "characterisation problem" for formal systems: the problem of finding "a necessary and sufficient condition that a formula of [formal system] F be a theorem of F." He writes:

> There is a trivial solution to the characterization problem for a theory T: a formula is a theorem iff it has a proof. This is an unsatisfactory solution because the condition for **A** to be a theorem depends upon all formulas which might appear in a proof of **A**. In a satisfactory solution, the condition must depend only upon **A** and formulas closely related to **A**.

An adaptation of Shoenfield's criterion to the characterisation of logic programming systems might be that the condition for a query **A** to succeed (fail) must depend only upon the conditions for success (failure) of **A** and formulae closely related to **A**.

Does SEQ meet this criterion? The compositional axioms certainly do, but what about the unfolding axioms? In support of the claim that they do is the fact that the unfoldings of **A** are classically equivalent to **A**, given the definitions in the program Π. The unfoldings of **A** also preserve much of the structure of **A**, changing only single predicate application subformulae or duplicating most of the formula. In this sense, we can say that the unfoldings of **A** are "closely related" to **A**.

On the other hand, they are not as closely related to **A** as we would expect given other logical systems. In traditional systems, the meaning of a formula is dependent only on the meanings of its immediate subformulae, possibly (in the case of the quantifiers) with a substitution applied to them. Whether we can come up with logical characterisations of sequential logic programming that more closely approximate this ideal is an open problem.

A related question is the following: do the operational and denotational semantics of sequential logic programming given in the past meet Shoenfield's criterion? These semantics are certainly "compositional" in the sense used to discuss denotational semantics: the denotation of a formula is a function of the denotations of its immediate subformulae. However, the success or failure of a query depends not on that of its subformulae, but on the properties of its denotation, which can be computed only by a process similar to computations in the operational semantics. It is difficult to say, therefore, that these semantics truly meet Shoenfield's criterion.

Of particular importance here is the reification of unification in denotational semantics of Prolog. Unification is an important algorithm which logic programmers must understand to know how their programs work. But it is used in the resolution method to solve a particular, important problem – the problem of finding witnesses for quantified variables. The primacy of the logical semantics of the existential quantifier remains.

It is this logical semantics – that the quantified formula is true (false) iff there is (is not) a witness – that is captured better by SEQ.

This is not to say that there are no other criteria for judging semantics, on which denotational semantics may be judged superior. Compositional, fully abstract denotational semantics have been extensively studied and are well understood. In some denotational semantics of Prolog, the cut and negation-as-failure operations are able to be described; in the formulation of logic programming that I use here, cut is not even definable and negation is not considered.

Whether denotational semantics will lead us to a logical characterisation of cut and negation as failure within the context of sequential logic programming remains to be seen, however. Future directions for the work in this chapter include an account of some form of negation and an if-then-else construct; see Chapter 6 for more details.

7.2. The Inversion Principle for SEQ

The Inversion Principle for natural deduction systems [63] can be phrased as follows: the elimination rules (in our context, the antecedent rules) for a connective should allow us to extract all of the information about a formula **A** that would be necessary to allow us to conclude that **A** was true. This is not the case for the left-hand rules for $S(\exists)$ and

$F(\&)$.

In the case of $S(\exists)$, for instance, we can conclude from the information that $\exists\mathbf{x}\ \mathbf{B}$ succeeds that there is a $\mathbf{t}$ such that $\mathbf{B}[\mathbf{x} := \mathbf{t}]$ succeeds. However, this information is not sufficient to prove that $\exists\mathbf{x}\ \mathbf{B}$ succeeds. This is one of the effects of having the non-compositional rules of predicate and disjunctive unfolding: the completeness of the consequent rules depends on being able to transform a formula into one for which certain side-conditions are met. In this case, we can regain the inversion property by making the same restriction on the formula as holds in the introduction rule: that $\mathbf{B}$ contain no predicate calls. If $\mathbf{B}$ does contain predicate calls, then we must use the antecedent unfolding rule, just as we have to use the consequent unfolding rule when the formula appears in the consequent.

The case of $F(\&)$ is more problematic. We cannot make the restriction that $\mathbf{B}$ contain no predicate calls, because it may be that $\mathbf{B}$ contains predicate calls but fails before it makes any. One possibility for regaining an inversion property is to split the left-hand axiom into two:

$$F(\mathbf{B}\&\mathbf{C}) \rightarrow F^N(\mathbf{B}) \vee F(\mathbf{A}')$$

where $\mathbf{B}$ contains predicate calls, and $\mathbf{A}'$ is a predicate unfolding of $(\mathbf{B}\&\mathbf{C})$; and

$$F(\mathbf{B}\&\mathbf{C}) \rightarrow F(\mathbf{B}) \vee (S(\mathbf{B})\&F(\mathbf{C}))$$

where $\mathbf{B}$ contains no predicate calls. These rules are slightly clumsy, but do extract as much information out of antecedent signed formulae as possible.

In short, we can modify some of the rules in SEQ to regain an inversion property. Since this involves making changes and restrictions to the rules inessential to the proofs of soundness and completeness, I chose not to make these restrictions in SEQ for simplicity's sake.

Chapter 5

Approaches to Incompleteness

Although we have proven some useful completeness theorems about the proof systems in the last two chapters, we have not been able to prove absolute completeness: that every valid sequent is derivable. Because of some formal incompleteness results, we will never be able to prove such a completeness theorem, for any finitary proof system; but there are several ways in which we can, at least partially, escape the effect of these incompleteness results. In this chapter, I present the incompleteness theorems and some of the partial solutions.

There are two main incompleteness results, as discussed in the first section below. The first says that we will never be able to derive all valid closed sequents which have signed formulae in negative contexts, and follows from the non-existence of a solution to the Halting Problem. (We can deal with many of the important cases of this result by adding extra rules which I will describe.) The second result says that we will never be able to derive all valid sequents with free variables, even if they have no signed formulae in negative contexts, and is a version of Gödel's Incompleteness Theorem.

The "mathematical" solution to these problems is to bring the proof theory closer to a kind of model theory, by allowing infinitary elements into the proof systems. Though these are not adequate solutions for practical theorem proving, they are useful in that they shed light on the extent to which the proof systems in question *are* complete. I discuss these methods in the second section of this chapter.

The more practical solution to some of the incompleteness problems is to add some form of induction. Many of the useful sequents with free variables which we cannot prove in the finitary systems in the last two chapters, can be proven if we add induction rules to the systems. Some of the variations on this approach are described in the last section.

1. Incompleteness

In the Closed Completeness results in the last two chapters, there were two restrictions on the class of valid sequents being proven derivable. The first was that signed formulae were barred from appearing in negative contexts; the second was that free variables were barred from appearing within signed formulae.

This is not to say that no valid sequent not appearing in the classes mentioned is derivable; many are, as for instance the Flat Completeness results show. So we can relax these restrictions to some extent, and show that wider classes of valid sequents are derivable. But we cannot remove either of them completely, even while maintaining the other. If we remove the first restriction, we will not be able to find a finitary proof system which is complete for that class of sequents, due to the unsolvability of the Halting Problem. This will also happen if we remove the second restriction, due this time to a version of Gödel's Incompleteness Theorem.

This section proves these incompleteness results, and points out a small relaxation of the first condition which will allow us to prove the derivability of another fairly useful class of valid sequents.

1.1. The Halting Problem and Divergence

If we maintain the restriction to closed sequents, can we relax the restriction to signed formulae only in positive contexts? The answer is no: although a finitary proof system (a proof system in which all judgments and derivations are of finite size) can be complete for closed sequents of the form $[\rightarrow S(\mathbf{A})]$ and $[\rightarrow F(\mathbf{A})]$, it cannot be complete for closed sequents in general.

Halting Problem Incompleteness

Theorem 1.1 (Halting Problem Incompleteness) There is no sound, finitary proof system for sequents (as defined in this thesis) which has as theorems all valid, closed sequents of the forms $[S(\mathbf{A}) \rightarrow]$ and $[F^Y(\mathbf{A}) \rightarrow]$; and this is the case for validity with respect to any variant of SOS.

Proof : The theorems of a finitary proof system can be recursively enumerated. If there were a sound, finitary proof system with the stated completeness property, then we would be able to effectively decide whether a given closed query $\mathbf{A}$ terminates or not. The procedure is as follows: dovetail the computations for enumerating the theorems of the forms $[S(\mathbf{B}) \rightarrow]$ and $[F^Y(\mathbf{B}) \rightarrow]$, and for enumerating the theorems of LKE+PAR (or LKE+SEQ or LKE+PASO) of the forms $[\rightarrow S(\mathbf{B})]$ and $[\rightarrow F^Y(\mathbf{B})]$. If $\mathbf{A}$ succeeds as a query, $[\rightarrow S(\mathbf{A})]$ will be reached eventually; if $\mathbf{A}$ fails, $[\rightarrow F^Y(\mathbf{A})]$ will be reached; and if $\mathbf{A}$ diverges, both $[S(\mathbf{A}) \rightarrow]$ and $[F^Y(\mathbf{A}) \rightarrow]$ will be reached. Stop when one of these situations arises.

Since every variant of SOS is Turing-complete, this procedure would constitute a solution to the halting problem. Therefore there can be no such proof system. □

Guaranteed Termination

The Halting Problem Incompleteness theorem seems a little "unfair" in some ways. Some sequents are valid for the trivial reason that some instance of some signed formula in a negative context diverges. It seems that many of the cases in which we will be unable to prove a valid sequent happen when the sequent is of this form. This is unfair because in practice, we will seldom want to prove such sequents; we are more interested in proving properties of programs given known success or failure properties of predicates.

One important class of such sequents has assumptions of the form $S(\mathbf{A})$ or $F(\mathbf{A})$, in which each instance of $\mathbf{A}$ either succeeds or fails. For instance, we may want to prove the sequent

$$S(Even(x)) \rightarrow S(N(x))$$

where N tests whether its argument is a Peano integer, and *Even* tests whether it is an even Peano integer. Every closed instance of this sequent is derivable in LKE+PAR or LKE+SEQ, even though the Closed Completeness theorem does not include it. In general, if we want to prove properties of predicates based on this kind of "type" or "structural" properties of their arguments, we will get sequents of this form. We would therefore like to prove a completeness result which takes in this class of sequents as well.

Definition 1.2 A goal formula **A** is *guaranteed terminating* (in a variant of SOS) if every instance of **A** either succeeds or fails. We similarly say that a signed formula is guaranteed terminating if its formula is guaranteed terminating.

To facilitate the proof of completeness for guaranteed termination, I will introduce two simple rules which are sound with respect to any operational semantics, but were not needed for proving soundness or completeness results so far. The completeness of guaranteed termination could be proven without them, but not without repeating many of the cases in the other completeness proofs. Let the set of rules GT be the following:

GT,S: $$\frac{\Gamma \rightarrow F^Y(\mathbf{A}), \Delta}{\Gamma, S(\mathbf{A}) \rightarrow \Delta}$$ GT,F: $$\frac{\Gamma \rightarrow S(\mathbf{A}), \Delta}{\Gamma, F(\mathbf{A}) \rightarrow \Delta}$$

where F in GT,F means either F^Y or F^N.

Theorem 1.3 The GT rules are sound with respect to any variant of SOS; that is, if the premisses of an application of one of the GT rules are valid wrt the variant, then the conclusion is valid wrt the variant.

Proof : Consider GT,S. The premiss says that if all the Γ assertions are valid under θ, then either $\mathbf{A}\theta$ fails (in which case $S(\mathbf{A})\theta$ is invalid and the conclusion is valid) or else one of the Δ assertions is valid under θ (in which case, again, the conclusion is valid).

The proof for GT,F is similar; the reasoning is the same for both the F^Y and F^N cases.
□

The kind of completeness that these rules give us is the following consequence of Closed Completeness, stage 3.

Theorem 1.4 (Completeness for Guaranteed Termination) All sequents S valid wrt SOS (resp. SP, SOS/so) in which all assertions in the antecedent are equality formulae or guaranteed-terminating signed formulae, all assertions in the consequent are equality formulae or signed formulae, and no free variable appears within an S or F^Y sign, are derivable in LKE+PAR+GT (resp. LKE+SEQ+GT, LKE+PASO+GT).

Proof : By induction on the number of signed formulae in the antecedent. When this is not zero, consider the first such formula, $\sigma(\mathbf{A})$. **A** either succeeds or fails; therefore (by Closed Completeness, stage 3) we can prove the sequent $[\rightarrow S(\mathbf{A}), F^Y(\mathbf{A})]$.

If σ is S, let S' be S with $S(\mathbf{A})$ removed from the antecedent and $F^Y(\mathbf{A})$ added to the consequent. S' is derivable from S using Cut and $[\rightarrow S(\mathbf{A}), F^Y(\mathbf{A})$, so it is valid; by the induction hypothesis, it must be derivable; and S is derivable from it by an application of the GT, S rule.

The cases where σ is F^Y or F^N are similar. □

There is a further result corresponding to stage 4 of Closed Completeness.

Theorem 1.5 All sequents $\mathcal{S}$ valid wrt SOS (resp. SP, SOS/so) in which no free variable appears in an S or F^Y subassertion, and no signed formula appears in a negative context *except* guaranteed-terminating signed formulae, are derivable in LKE+PAR+GT (resp. LKE+SEQ+GT, LKE+PASO+GT).

Proof : As in the previous two chapters. □

With the guaranteed-termination rules, we therefore have the ability to derive some important valid sequents. We cannot yet derive $S(Even(x)) \rightarrow S(N(x))$, since this contains free variables, but we can derive every instance of it.

Of course, with guaranteed termination, we still have the problem of actually guaranteeing the termination! We need to prove, essentially, that $[\rightarrow S(\mathbf{A}), F(\mathbf{A})]$ is valid, for each $\sigma(\mathbf{A})$ appearing in a negative context. If such a sequent is closed or has no recursive predicates, then (by the completeness results) we can give a derivation for it. Otherwise, we may need to prove its validity by hand – or use the induction rules given in the last section of this chapter to derive it.

1.2. Gödel Incompleteness

In this section, I give a sketch of a proof that there is no sound, complete, finitary proof system for sequents without the restriction on free variables, even retaining the restriction against having signed formulae in a negative context. This proof is a variant of Gödel's proof of the incompleteness of arithmetic [39]. For simplicity, the exact version of the theorem I will prove will be about different kinds of judgements than sequents. I trust that this will convince readers of the truth of the more specific theorem. The theorem applies to validity with respect to any variant of SOS.

Definition 1.6 A *program-formula judgement* in a language $\mathcal{L}$ is an expression of the form $\langle \Pi, \sigma(\mathbf{A}) \rangle$, where Π is (some syntactic representation of) a program in $\mathcal{L}$, and $\sigma(\mathbf{A})$ is a signed formula of $\mathcal{L}$.

A judgement $\langle \Pi, \sigma(\mathbf{A}) \rangle$ is *valid* with respect to some variant of SOS if every closed instance of $\sigma(\mathbf{A})$ is valid with respect to that variant of SOS, and to the program Π.

Theorem 1.7 (Incompleteness) For some language $\mathcal{L}$, there is no sound, complete, and finitary proof system S with program-formula judgements. That is, for every sound and finitary proof system S with program-formula judgements, there is some such judgement that is valid but not derivable in S.

Proof : Assume that, for every $\mathcal{L}$, there is such a proof system; then prove a contradiction.

Choose $\mathcal{L}$ so that we can represent variables, terms, formulae, signed formulae, finite programs, judgements, and derivations for such a proof system, all as closed terms. As Gödel showed, any language with at least one nullary function symbol and at least one non-nullary function symbol suffices. Applying the assumption, we have a sound and complete finitary proof system S for judgements in this language. We can decide on a representation within the language of each expression (variable, term, etc.); let us write $\lceil \mathbf{X} \rceil$ for the representation of the expression $\mathbf{X}$.

The readers can convince themselves that we can write a program Π_G containing predicates *Subst* and *Deriv* with the following operational properties:

- The closed query $Subst(\mathbf{r}, \mathbf{s}_1, \mathbf{s}_2, \mathbf{t})$ succeeds iff $\mathbf{r}$ is some $\lceil\sigma(\mathbf{A})\rceil$, and we can obtain $\mathbf{t}$ from $\mathbf{r}$ by substituting all occurrences of $\lceil z_1\rceil$ by $\mathbf{s}_1$ and all occurrences of $\lceil z_2\rceil$ by $\mathbf{s}_2$. (Note that z_1, z_2 are fixed variable names.) Moreover, if $\mathbf{r}, \mathbf{s}_1, \mathbf{s}_2$ are all closed and $\mathbf{t}$ is some variable $\mathbf{x}$, then the query does not fail, and the resultant substitution substitutes a closed term for $\mathbf{x}$.
- The closed query $Deriv(\mathbf{r}, \mathbf{s}, \mathbf{t})$ succeeds iff $\mathbf{s}$ is some $\lceil\Pi\rceil$, $\mathbf{t}$ is some $\lceil\sigma(\mathbf{A})\rceil$, and $\mathbf{r}$ is the representation of a derivation, in the proof system S, of $\langle\Pi, \sigma(\mathbf{A})\rangle$. Moreover, if all the arguments are closed terms, then the query terminates (either succeeds or fails).

(Note that we can write these predicates so that they behave properly under any variant of SOS.)

Now, let U be the signed formula

$$F(\exists y(Subst(z_2, z_1, z_2, y)\&Deriv(x, z_1, y)))$$

Let G be the signed formula $U[z_1 := \lceil\Pi_G\rceil, z_2 := \lceil U\rceil]$; that is, let G be

$$F(\exists y(Subst(\lceil U\rceil, \lceil\Pi_G\rceil, \lceil U\rceil, y)\&Deriv(x, \lceil\Pi_G\rceil, y)))$$

Is $\langle\Pi_G, G\rangle$ derivable in S? If so, then it must be valid, since S is sound. Therefore G is valid with respect to Π; that is, for any closed term $\mathbf{t}$ we substitute in for x in G, we have that the query

$$(\exists y(Subst(\lceil U\rceil, \lceil\Pi_G\rceil, \lceil U\rceil, y)\&Deriv(\mathbf{t}, \lceil\Pi_G\rceil, y))) \qquad (*)$$

fails. However, the call to Subst cannot fail, and must in fact produce a substitution mapping y to some closed term $\mathbf{s}$.

But what is this closed term $\mathbf{s}$? It is in fact $\lceil G\rceil$. From this we must conclude that the query $Deriv(\mathbf{t}, \lceil\Pi_G\rceil, \lceil G\rceil)$ fails, for every $\mathbf{t}$. But what this means is that there is no derivation for $\langle\Pi_G, G\rangle$, even though that was what we just assumed. Thus, $\langle\Pi_G, G\rangle$ must not be derivable in S after all.

However, it is still the case that the call to Subst cannot fail, and that the call to Deriv cannot diverge; so the query $(*)$ must fail, for every choice of $\mathbf{t}$. This means that $\langle\Pi_G, G\rangle$ is in fact valid but underivable.

This contradicts our first assumption that S was complete; so for this choice of $\mathcal{L}$, there can be no sound, complete, and finitary proof system for program-formula judgements. □

The kind of proof systems we have been studying in the other chapters are parameterised by the (implicit) program: that is, there is a different proof system for each program. This parameterisation was done only for convenience, however, and we could instead give calculi whose judgements are sequents with appended programs. It should be clear that the incompleteness proof will still apply to the parameterised proof systems, as long as they are still finitary.

2. Infinitary Methods

The incompleteness results of the last section emphasised the restriction to *finitary* proof systems: proof systems with judgments and derivations which can be represented finitely.

Although these are really the only kinds of proof systems which can be used in practice, it is possible to obtain much stronger completeness results by adding infinitary elements to the system.

Of course, if our only concern had been to build a finitary proof system, and we now had decided to remove that restriction, we could simply code the entire operational semantics and definition of validity into a complete "proof system". We must take care to adhere to our original goals of producing as logical a proof system as possible, and not to add elements which are so strong as to make the proof system trivially complete. Infinitary methods meeting these criteria are the addition of an infinitary rule (rule with an infinite number of premisses) to handle free variables in sequents, and the addition of elements to handle divergence by model checking methods.

2.1. An Infinitary Rule for Free Variables

In the study of program logics, infinitary rules are often introduced to handle free variables [40]. The technique involves adding a single, simple rule which infers the validity of an assertion from the validity of all its (possibly infinite number of) closed instances. Many useful results follow from this addition – enough to justify the theoretical study of the augmented system.

Consider the following rule:

$$\text{Inf: } \frac{\Gamma[\mathbf{x} := \mathbf{t}_1] \rightarrow \Delta[\mathbf{x} := \mathbf{t}_1] \quad \Gamma[\mathbf{x} := \mathbf{t}_2] \rightarrow \Delta[\mathbf{x} := \mathbf{t}_2] \quad \ldots}{\Gamma \rightarrow \Delta}$$

where $\mathbf{t}_1, \mathbf{t}_2, \ldots$ is an enumeration of all the closed terms in the language

If the language $\mathcal{L}$ has an infinite number of closed terms, then this rule has an infinite number of premisses. However, the addition of this rule allows us to remove the restriction to closed sequents in the various completeness proofs. The soundness of the infinitary rule follows immediately from the definition of validity, and we can prove (for instance) the following analogue of the Closed Completeness, stage 4 theorem for PAR:

Theorem 2.1 (Completeness of Infinitary System) All valid sequents S in which no signed formula appears in a negative context are derivable in LKE+PAR+Inf.

Proof : By induction on the total number of free variables which appear in S or F^Y formulae. Each free variable can be eliminated by one application of Inf. □

A more important "characterisation" corollary is the following.

Theorem 2.2 Every instance of a goal formula $\mathbf{A}$ succeeds in SOS iff the sequent $[\rightarrow S(\mathbf{A})]$ is derivable in LKE+PAR+Inf; every instance of it fails in SOS iff the sequent $[\rightarrow F^Y(\mathbf{A})]$ is derivable in LKE+PAR+Inf.

Proof : From the Soundness theorem for LKE+PAR+Inf and the Completeness theorem above. □

The analogous results also hold for LKE+SEQ+Inf, LKE+PASO+Inf, and any of these systems augmented by the Guaranteed Termination rules of the last section.

The value of this infinitary rule lies in its simplicity, combined with the scope of the resulting completeness. The importance of the infinitary rule is that it says something about the *other* rules in the given proof systems: it says that they are complete, "except that they cannot handle free variables." This is useful, since it assures us that the rules are not incomplete for some other reason, as for instance they would be if one of the connective axioms were missing. This complements the knowledge that we have from the Closed Completeness results that the finitary systems are complete for a wide class of closed sequents.

If we had the infinitary rule from the beginning, some of the completeness results would be easier to prove, since we could assume right from the start that all sequents were closed and introduce free variables only at the last stage. Some of the equality rules are redundant in the system with the infinitary rule. In fact, the two groups of equality rules in LKE represent those which would be needed even with unrestricted use of the infinitary rule (Eq, Ineq, and Comp), and those which serve to replace the infinitary rule to some extent in some of the completeness theorems for the finitary systems (Occ, Sub,l, and Sub,r).

Finally, the infinitary rule is very useful in smoothing out a difficulty with the completeness results. Note that the completeness theorem for equality (4.3) followed directly from the assumption that there was an infinite number of closed terms in the base language. Without this assumption, the theorem would not be true: there would be a valid sequent satisfying the restrictions in the theorems but underivable in LKE. For example, consider the language with only two terms, the constants a and b; then the sequent $[\rightarrow x = a, x = b]$ would be valid, since under any of the two minimal substitutions which make it closed ($[x := a]$ and $[x := b]$), one of its formulae is valid. All the other completeness theorems are based on this equality completeness theorem, so all these would fail as well.

However, the case in which there are only a finite number of terms is exactly the case in which the "infinitary" rule is no longer infinitary! Thus in this case we can prove the first stages of the completeness results in a trivial manner by using the "infinitary" rule, and the strong completeness theorem of this section can be proved without infinitary constructs.

2.2. Model Checking for Divergence

What about the other restriction in the Closed Completeness results, that arose from the inability to handle divergence? Can it be eliminated using infinitary methods?

It would take us outside the scope of this thesis, but it may be possible to develop a complete proof system based on model-checking techniques [15]. This would involve representations of (possibly infinite) models as part of the proof system.

There is also a body of literature on detecting infinite loops in Prolog programs, with varying degrees of formality of approach [61, 75, 8]. It may be possible to formalise one of these approaches within the context of the sequents defined here in order to obtain a finitary and more complete proof system.

3. Induction

The finitary proof systems of the last chapters are complete for all closed sequents with empty antecedents, and all sequents involving non-recursive predicates. However, there are many practically important non-closed assertions involving recursive predicates which cannot be proven by them; and needless to say, the infinitary techniques of the last section are not useful in practice.

The main finitary method of handling such assertions in practice is induction. This is a generalisation of the usual practice of proving a statement about the natural numbers using "mathematical induction": if the statement holds for 0, and whenever it holds for n it holds for $n+1$, then it holds for all natural numbers.

In the context of proof systems, we can add proof rules which formalise this method of reasoning. The two major types of induction rules that we might add are the simpler, but less general subterm induction rule, and the more complex but much more general and useful well-founded induction rule. Neither of these rules give us a complete proof system, because of Gödel incompleteness; but they do enable us to prove a useful subset of the non-closed sequents.

3.1. Subterm Induction

The proof rules formalising what I call "subterm induction" allow us to do only induction over the structure of terms. This is a common form of inductive reasoning about programs, first noted by Burstall [16]; it can be seen as a formal justification of such programming techniques as CDR'ing down a list, or tree traversal.

To introduce this idea, let us see how induction can be done in the context of the natural numbers. Takeuti [72] gives the following induction rule for natural numbers (in our notation):

$$\frac{\Gamma, \mathbf{A}(\mathbf{x}) \rightarrow \mathbf{A}(s(\mathbf{x})), \Delta}{\Gamma, \mathbf{A}(0) \rightarrow \mathbf{A}(\mathbf{t}), \Delta}$$

where $\mathbf{x}$ does not appear free in Γ, Δ or $\mathbf{A}(0)$.

This rule can be read as saying that if (a) whenever a formula $\mathbf{A}$ is true of some term $\mathbf{t}$ it is true of $s(\mathbf{t})$, and (b) $\mathbf{A}$ is true of 0, then we can conclude that it is true of every term. We can prove this rule sound, in the context of arithmetic, because the only basic term constructors we have are the constant 0 and the unary function symbol s. If we had more function symbols, the rule would not be sound because there is no guarantee that $\mathbf{A}$ is true for (for instance) some other constant.

One generalisation of this rule to take in arbitrary languages can be formulated as follows.

Definition 3.1 Let $\mathcal{S}$ be of the form $\Gamma \rightarrow \Delta, \sigma(\mathbf{A}(\mathbf{x}))$, where $\mathbf{A}(\mathbf{x})$ is the only formula in $\mathcal{S}$ to have $\mathbf{x}$ free. Let $\mathbf{f}$ be an n-ary function symbol. Then $IH(\mathcal{S}, \mathbf{f}, \mathbf{x})$ is the sequent

$$\Gamma, \sigma(\mathbf{A}(\mathbf{y}_1)), \ldots, \sigma(\mathbf{A}(\mathbf{y}_n)) \rightarrow \Delta, \sigma(\mathbf{A}(\mathbf{f}(\mathbf{y}_1, \ldots, \mathbf{y}_n)))$$

where $\mathbf{y}_1, \ldots, \mathbf{y}_n$ are n variables not free in $\mathcal{S}$.

The induction rule (or more properly rule schema) for the sequent calculus now takes the form

$$\frac{IH(\mathcal{S}, \mathbf{f}_1, \mathbf{x}) \quad \ldots \quad IH(\mathcal{S}, \mathbf{f}_m, \mathbf{x})}{\mathcal{S}}$$

where $\mathcal{S}$ is any sequent of the form $\Gamma \rightarrow \Delta, \sigma(\mathbf{A}(\mathbf{x}))$, $\mathbf{A}(\mathbf{x})$ is the only formula in $\mathcal{S}$ to have $\mathbf{x}$ free, and $\mathbf{f}_1 \ldots \mathbf{f}_m$ are all the function symbols in the language $\mathcal{L}$. This rule, which

I will call SUBTERM, is sound in the same sense that the other rules we have discussed are sound, as stated by the following theorem.

Theorem 3.2 If each premiss of an application of the induction rule is valid with respect to some variant of SOS, then the conclusion is valid with respect to it.

Proof : If $\Gamma \rightarrow \Delta$ is valid, then the result holds trivially. Otherwise, there is some substitution $\theta[\mathbf{x} := \mathbf{t}]$ under which all of the Γ signed formulae are valid, and we must prove that $\sigma(\mathbf{A})$ is valid under it. We can do this by induction on the structure of $\mathbf{t}$; each subcase corresponds to one of the premisses of the rule application. □

See Section 4. for an extended example of the use of subterm induction – a derivation of the sequent $[\rightarrow S(Add(x, 0, x))]$. It is possible to derive this sequent using the infinitary rule mentioned in the last section, but not with just the rules in the finitary proof systems of Chapters 3 and 4. Subterm induction allows us to derive it using only finitary methods.

3.2. Disadvantages of Subterm Induction

The advantage of subterm induction is that the rule is easily stated, and easily applied for simple languages. As the language increases in size, however, we begin to run into problems.

If we had other function symbols in the language – say the constant symbol a – example sequents such as the one above would not even be valid, because $Add(a, \mathbf{s}, \mathbf{t})$ fails for every $\mathbf{s}$ and $\mathbf{t}$. What would be valid is the sequent $[\rightarrow S(N(x)) \supset S(Add(x, 0, x))]$, where N is the predicate which checks whether its parameter is a Peano natural number:

$$N(x) \leftrightarrow x = 0 \vee \exists px(x = s(px) \& N(px))$$

This latter sequent we could prove using the induction rule. However, the premiss for the constant a would be $[\rightarrow S(N(a)) \supset S(Add(a, 0, a)]$, which would be valid only by virtue of $N(a)$ failing.

In general, as we add function symbols, we add premisses to the induction rule which we must prove in many trivial cases. This is a problem in general with logic programs, because we often want to prove properties about predicates while assuming some type information about the parameters to the predicate (e.g., that all parameters are lists), but we generally have many function symbols.

Another shortcoming of subterm induction is that not all recursions found in programs are on the subterm structure of the parameters to a predicate. Some predicates terminate in general because of some other decreasing measure. For assertions involving these predicates, we could define an natural number measure on the parameters and use subterm induction on natural numbers to derive the relevant sequents. This may turn out to be rather complicated, however; a more general solution is discussed in the next section.

If we were working with a strongly typed logic, in which all formulae, terms and variables have an associated type, some of these problems would vanish. In typed logic programming languages (and strongly typed programming languages in general [18]), the definition of a predicate includes a specification of the types of its arguments; calls to predicates with arguments of anything other than the correct types are syntactically ill-formed. The number of cases to consider in the induction rule would therefore not increase with bigger languages; for instance, one would specify that the arguments to *Add* were exclusively of natural number type, and only two premisses would ever be needed for the induction rule.

The addition of types to our language would take us outside the scope of this thesis, although some form of typing is clearly desirable, for this and other reasons. However, even in a typed language we are left with the problem of recursions which do not act on subterm structure. This problem must still be handled by a generalisation of induction to induction on any well-founded measure.

3.3. Well-Founded Induction

General *well-founded induction* [51] is more powerful (in the sense of allowing more proofs) and in some ways simpler than subterm induction. With well-founded induction, there is only one premiss to the induction rule, although this premiss depends on a metatheoretic proof of a property of a predicate.

Manna and Waldinger's formulation, from which this discussion is drawn, uses relations as part of the program logic. Because we are talking about logic programming, we can use object logic relations (the defined predicates of the program) as our well-founded order relations.

Definition 3.3 A predicate $\mathbf{R}$ defined in a program Π is *a well-ordering* in Π if:

- For no closed $\mathbf{t}$ does $\mathbf{R}(\mathbf{t},\mathbf{t})$ succeed; and
- There is no infinite sequence of closed terms $\mathbf{t}_1, \mathbf{t}_2, \mathbf{t}_3, \ldots$ such that $\mathbf{R}(\mathbf{t}_{i+1}, \mathbf{t}_i)$ succeeds for all $i \geq 1$ ("there is no infinite descending sequence of closed terms").

Using well-ordering predicates, we can define an induction rule, WF, which is in some ways simpler and more useful than that of the last section:

$$\frac{\Gamma, \forall \mathbf{x}(S(\mathbf{R}(\mathbf{x},\mathbf{y})) \supset \mathbf{A}(\mathbf{x})) \rightarrow \mathbf{A}(\mathbf{y}), \Delta}{\Gamma \rightarrow \mathbf{A}(\mathbf{y}), \Delta}$$

where $\mathbf{R}$ is a well-ordering and $\mathbf{y}$ does not appear free in Γ or Δ. (Note that the proof that $\mathbf{R}$ is a well-ordering cannot be done within the proof system, and must be done metatheoretically.)

The definition of well-ordering could be made more straightforward by our insisting that, for instance, $\mathbf{R}(\mathbf{t},\mathbf{t})$ fail. However, the weaker conditions above suffice to ensure the soundness of the well-founded induction rule.

Theorem 3.4 If the premiss of an application of the well-founded induction rule is valid (with respect to some variant of SOS), then the conclusion is valid (with respect to that variant of SOS).

Proof : By reductio ad absurdum. Call $\mathbf{t}$ a *counterexample* for an assertion $\mathbf{B}(\mathbf{x})$ with free variable $\mathbf{x}$ if $\mathbf{B}(\mathbf{t})$ is invalid.

Assume the premiss is valid but the conclusion is invalid. (This is the reductio assumption.) This means that there is a $\theta[\mathbf{y} := \mathbf{t}_1]$ which makes the conclusion closed, such that all its antecedent assertions are valid under $\theta[\mathbf{y} := \mathbf{t}_1]$ but none of its consequent assertions (including $\mathbf{A}(\mathbf{y})$) is valid under $\theta[\mathbf{y} := \mathbf{t}_1]$. (In other words, $\mathbf{t}_1$ is a counterexample for $\mathbf{A}(\mathbf{y})\theta$.) However, by assumption, the premiss is valid; so since none of *its* consequent assertions are valid under $\theta[\mathbf{y} := \mathbf{t}_1]$, one of its antecedent assertions must be invalid under $\theta[\mathbf{y} := \mathbf{t}_1]$; and the only one that can be is $\forall\mathbf{x}(S(\mathbf{R}(\mathbf{x},\mathbf{y})) \supset \mathbf{A}(\mathbf{x}))$. Since this is invalid under $\theta[\mathbf{y} := \mathbf{t}_1]$, there must be a $\mathbf{t}_2$ such that $(S(\mathbf{R}(\mathbf{x},\mathbf{y})) \supset \mathbf{A}(\mathbf{x}))[\mathbf{x} := \mathbf{t}_2]\theta[\mathbf{y} := \mathbf{t}_1]$ is invalid; that is, such that $\mathbf{R}(\mathbf{t}_2, \mathbf{t}_1)$ succeeds but $(\mathbf{A}(\mathbf{t}_2))\theta$ is invalid.

But this would mean that $\mathbf{t}_2$, like $\mathbf{t}_1$, is also a counterexample for $\mathbf{A}(\mathbf{y})\theta$, and since $\mathbf{R}$ is a well-ordering, $\mathbf{t}_2$ must be distinct from $\mathbf{t}_1$. So we can follow the same line of reasoning to get another counterexample $\mathbf{t}_3$ such that $\mathbf{R}(\mathbf{t}_3, \mathbf{t}_2)$ succeeds, and so on. But then we will have the infinite descending sequence of closed terms which we denied we had when we assumed $\mathbf{R}$ was a well-ordering. Contradiction; so the conclusion of the application of the rule must be valid after all. □

With well-founded induction, we can prove all of the things we could with subterm induction (since the subterm inclusion predicate is a well-ordering), but in some situations the derivations are simpler. Consider the sequent $[\rightarrow S(N(x)) \supset S(Add(x, 0, x))]$, which was easy to prove with only two function symbols in the language, but became more cumbersome as the number of symbols increased. With well-founded induction, the complexity of the derivation is large, but the derivation is independent of the number of function symbols in the language. One possibility for a well-ordering predicate is the predicate R given by the following definitions:

$$R(x, y) \leftrightarrow N(x)\&N(y)\&Lt(x, y)$$

$$Lt(x, y) \leftrightarrow \exists py(y = s(py)\&(x = py \vee Lt(x, py)))$$

In the new derivation, the assumption in R that x is a natural number cancels the assumption $N(x)$ in the assertion to be proved, and the derivation has no more branches than did the subterm induction derivation. This derivation is also in the Appendix.

The main disadvantage of well-founded induction is that the order relation must be formulated, proven well-founded, and (in our formulation) defined in the program. This is quite tedious, especially if the order relation is of the simple kind given in the example above. There should be some way of automatically generating order relations from given type assumptions which will allow us to prove assertions involving those type assumptions. As with the corresponding problem with subterm induction, an explicit type system in our logic would help here.

Chapter 6

Summary and Future Directions

This thesis has taken as its object of study the control-discipline variants of a simple logic programming language equivalent to Horn clause logic programming. It has classified and logically characterised the set of successful and failing queries of these variants of the language.

I have given an operational semantics, SOS, of which variants correspond to the parallel "and" and "or", sequential "and", sequential "or", and sequential "and" and "or" control disciplines. This operational semantics homogenises the treatment of the control disciplines by incorporating control information (such as the failure-backtrack mechanism of seqeuntial systems) into the operational semantics. (Some of the variants of SOS have equivalent compositional operational semantics, which I have given.) I have also classified the queries into those succeeding and those failing in each of the control disciplines, and have proven the equivalence of some of these classes.

I have then used a sequent calculus framework, in which the elements of sequents are assertions about the success or failure of queries, to give a logical analysis of these classes of queries. Three calculi are given; they share a common set LKE of rules for classical logic with equality as syntactic identity, and differ in the set of axioms which characterise the behaviour of queries.

- LKE+PAR characterises the queries which succeed in parallel-or systems, and those which fail in parallel-and systems;
- LKE+SEQ characterises the queries which succeed in the sequential-and, sequential-or system, and those which fail in sequential-and systems;
- LKE+PASO characterises the queries which succeed in the parallel-and, sequential-or system.

The precise sense in which these calculi "characterise" the classes of queries is that if a query succeeds or fails in a particular control discipline, the corresponding assertion of its success or failure is derivable in the appropriate calculus. The value of these characterisations is that they give a precise, logical account of which queries fail or succeed.

These calculi can also be used for proving more general properties of logic programs, including general termination and correctness properties. This is important, as it addresses issues of program correctness and specification which arise in practical settings. The sequent calculi can therefore act as a basis for practical tools for proving such properties of programs. See below for a more detailed discussion of this possibility.

The sequents of the calculi are sufficiently expressive that the calculi cannot be complete with respect to the natural notion of validity; but I have shown several results that give a wide range of valid, derivable sequents. I have also analysed the senses in which the systems in question must be incomplete, and have given extensions, such as induction rules, which can be used to prove a wide class of useful properties of programs.

1. Language Extensions

One of the main deficiencies of this thesis, from a practical point of view, is that the programming language it considers is not very expressive or powerful. Logic programs as I have defined them are a variant of the strict Horn clause programs originally described by Kowalski [49]. Since then, the state of the art has moved on considerably. It would be desirable to incorporate more recent developments into the language being characterised, to see whether they can be treated in the proof-theoretic framework given in this thesis.

1.1. Iterated Implication and Universal Quantification

As Gabbay and Reyle [35] and Miller and Nadathur [55] have shown, it is possible to add implication and universal quantification to the class of goal formulae, in restricted contexts, and get a logic programming language which has a reasonable operational semantics. The resulting language allows many useful programming constructs, including the incremental buildup of the definition of a predicate, module definitions, and variable scoping. For instance, if D_1, D_2 and D_3 are conjunctions of predicate declarations and G_1 and G_2 are goals, then the goal $D_1 \supset (D_2 \supset G_1)\&(D_3 \supset G_2)$ indicates that the system is to search for a solution to G_1 in the context of the program $D_1\&D_2$, and for a solution to G_2 in the context of the program $D_1\&D_3$.

Can languages such as that specified by hereditary Harrop formulae (or languages with similar iterated implication and universal quantification constructs) be analysed within the proof-theoretic framework? It may be possible, but it may require a more complex form of signed formula, and the treatment of sequentiality may be more problematic.

To give a proof-theoretic characterisation similar to those in this thesis, it seems that signed formulae must be of the form $\sigma^{\Pi}(\mathbf{A})$, where Π is a program, since the program can change during the course of a computation. Because of the possible incremental buildup of the program, we must abandon the bi-implicative form of predicate definition, and stay with the definition of a program as a hereditary Harrop definition.

The operational semantics given by Miller et al. [55] is nondeterministic, and so specifies a parallel discipline; for a sequential interpreter, one would have to assume something about the order in which clauses are added to the program (at the end?), and possibly construct the Clark completion of a predicate definition whenever a predicate expansion is performed.

1.2. Types

Types are important in any programming language. Their main practical use is to allow programmers to specify what kinds of arguments they expect predicates (or functions or procedures) to take, so that the compiler or interpreter can inform programmers of inconsistencies in use of predicates. In large programs, this can be very helpful, as this kind of type inconsistency is a common source of errors and can be checked relatively cheaply.

Types would also be important in facilitating inductive proofs of properties of logic programs. As suggested in Section 3., it may be possible to give simpler rules for subterm induction over given types, and the presence of types can considerably simplify the statements of theorems to be proven (as all type assumptions are implicit in the predicate applications being made). To do induction over the structure of a given free variable, one would choose the appropriate rule for that variable, eliminating the need for vacuous premisses corresponding to incorrectly-typed terms and reducing the need for well-ordering predicates for well-founded induction.

The question of how we should add types to logic programming languages is an area of current research [64, 65]. An important question would be which of the currently-proposed type systems would be best suited to proof-theoretic analysis.

1.3. Variable Modes

In logic programming, variable mode declarations on predicate arguments are arguably as important as type declarations. A variable mode declaration [28] is a declaration of how instantiated the programmer expects an argument to be when the predicate is called or when it returns; examples of modes include "var" (the parameter is an unbound variable), "nonvar" (the parameter may be partially instantiated), and "ground" (the parameter is fully instantiated).

Like type declarations, mode declarations can be used by programmers to enlist the help of the compiler or interpreter to check that a predicate is used as expected. However, there are other uses of modes. Modes allow us to optimise unifications in a goal or program; for instance, in a computation of $x = y$ where y is of "ground" mode, the unification is at worst a matching (for which very fast algorithms are known) and at best, when x is of "var" mode, a simple assignment. Modes thus also allow us to identify classes of predicates which can be compiled or interpreted efficiently. These ideas are implemented in Paul Voda's language Trilogy [2].

As might be suggested by the completeness proofs in this thesis, information that a variable represents a ground term is useful in proving assertions. Plümer [60, 59] has used mode information to prove termination of logic programs, for the more limited notion of termination in which all solutions can be found finitely. Some of his techniques might be formalisable within the framework of a sequent calculus.

Finally, when programmers have the ability to specify modes, language designers have the ability to insist that only variables with certain modes be used in certain contexts. As we will see below, this can be used to add new features to the language, such as negation, which can be implemented in a more efficient and complete manner with mode information.

Other modes, and variations on the definition of mode, have been given in the literature [28, 31]. Which definitions would go best with the proof-theoretic technique is a topic which deserves investigation.

1.4. Predicate Names as Terms

Several extensions to logic programming have been proposed which move it into the realm of higher order logic [55, 19]. I have explored one such simple extension [3], in which predicate names are treated as atomic terms, in a simpler setting than the one in this thesis; viewing it in a sequent calculus setting raises interesting questions.

The extension is based on Gilmore's nominalistic set theory NaDSet [37]. Besides treating predicate names as terms, the extension allows any term to appear where only a predicate name can appear in first order logic programming. (It also makes several other extensions which are unimportant for this discussion.) The operational semantics given in [3] is nondeterministic, that is, parallel-and and parallel-or; the proof-theoretic characterisation is a natural deduction proof system for successful queries. These systems should be easy to cast into the *parallel* SOS and sequent calculus framework.

However, when we consider issues of sequentiality, problems arise. Consider the query $\exists x(x(3) \mathbin{\&} false \mathbin{\&} x = P)$, where P is some predicate name. The nondeterministic (parallel) operational semantics fails on this query. If we sequentialised the operational semantics in the natural way – computing the conjuncts from left to right – the query would fail in the sequential system too. Neither system would evaluate the query in such a way as to require that $P(3)$ be computed, instead deferring the computation until x is bound or the query fails. However, we cannot use the rules for failing existential and conjunctive queries from SEQ here, because that would require a proof that $(P(3) \mathbin{\&} false \mathbin{\&} P = P)$ fails – which may not be true in the sequential system since P might diverge.

This problem has some of the flavour of the disjunction problem which caused us to introduce disjunctive unfoldings. It may therefore be solvable by a similar technique. It may, however, be easier to add this feature to a language which already has variable mode declarations. Then, we could restrict occurrences of variables in predicate positions to those declared to be of "ground" mode. This would exclude the query given above, but still include many of the useful predicates which we want to write in a higher order setting.

1.5. Negation and If-Then-Else

Negation was one of the first features that researchers attempted to add to Horn clause logic programming, and has remained one of the most problematic. In the proof-theoretic setting, we would naturally like to have axioms like $S(\neg\mathbf{A}) \leftrightarrow F(\mathbf{A})$ and $F(\neg\mathbf{A}) \leftrightarrow S(\mathbf{A})$. Whether we can achieve this depends strongly on the operational treatment of negation.

I will not attempt to review the extensive work done on the semantics of negation in Prolog. I will simply point out that not all of the work on negation in sequential languages would necessarily mesh well with the analysis in this thesis. For instance, in Naish's MU-Prolog [56], the computation of non-ground negated subgoals is delayed until they are ground, or until there are only non-ground negated subgoals left. Essentially, subgoals are re-ordered as the computation progresses. This strategy, while practically very useful, would play havoc with attempts at giving a logical characterisation of the exact set of failing and successful queries along the lines of this thesis.

As with predicates-as-terms, variable mode declarations might enable us to give a reasonable account of negation. We could insist that all variables appearing in negated goal formulae be of "ground" mode, and use negation as failure for the allowed occurrences of negation. In this way, we can capture a large class of uses of negation without sacrificing logicality; as Jaffar et al. have shown [47], negation as failure is a complete strategy for ground negated queries.

Some form of if-then-else construct would also be possible if we used modes in this way. The expression **if A then B else C** could be defined as being equivalent to $(\mathbf{A}\&\mathbf{B}) \vee (\neg\mathbf{A}\&\mathbf{C})$, if we maintain the syntactic restriction of **A** to having only input-mode free variables.

In an if-then-else formula, the condition **A** need be computed only once. It is therefore better to have an explicit if-then-else construct than to just write the equivalent formula, since it not only clarifies the underlying meaning of the formula, but also signals to the compiler or interpreter that this optimisation can be done. A bonus of such an if-then-else construct is that it can be used to replace many uses of the non-logical Prolog "cut", which is commonly used to avoid having to compute the negation of a positive condition in another clause.

1.6. Constraints

The area of constraints seems promising as a possible extension to the framework in this thesis. This is because constraint logic programming languages generally extend basic logic programming in ways which are independent of the various control disciplines.

One description of a subset of the constraint logic programming languages is as follows. We are given a first order language $\mathcal{L}$, with some predicate names in $\mathcal{L}$ being identified as *constraint predicates.* We are also given a semantics for these constraint predicates – a characterisation of which applications of the constraint predicates are considered to be true and which false. (How many of the useful CLP languages described by Jaffar and Lassez [46] this description captures is not clear.)

In conventional logic programming (which is subsumed by the constraint paradigm), the only constraint predicate is equality, which is interpreted as syntactic identity. But other systems are possible: for instance, the addition of $\neq$ as a constraint predicate [1], the interpretation of $=$ as identity between infinite rational trees [25], Presburger arithmetic, and linear arithmetic [46].

In the sequent-calculus framework of this thesis, none of these languages would seem to require anything more than an axiomatisation of the semantics of the constraint predicates, along the lines of the axiomatisation of equality in LKE. On the operational semantics side, we need, for each constraint language, a unification (or "subsumption") algorithm which allows us to completely decide whether a given finite set of constraint predicate applications is satisfiable or not.

Because of the requirement that a subsumption algorithm exist, one would expect that the entire analysis of successful and failing queries for both parallel and sequential systems would go through as in this thesis. In particular, there would be analogues of the Equality Completeness theorem (4.3) which would form the basis of the rest of the completeness theorems; the remainder of the theorems are mainly about the connectives and defined predicates, and so would go through as before.

1.7. Multiple Control Disciplines

As mentioned in Chapter 2, most practical languages which have parallel "and" and "or" also have the sequential versions of these connectives. It would be useful to have a language in which all four connectives (parallel and sequential "and" and "or") were represented, and the associated operational semantics and proof theory.

The proof theory would seem to be straightforward; it should be just the amalgamation of all of the rules from PAR and SEQ, with the success axioms for conjunction from PAR becoming axioms for the parallel "and", and so on. What would be more difficult is the operational semantics. The interaction of the four connectives is sufficiently complex that it does not seem to fit easily into any of the styles of semantics given in Chapter 2. Voda [76] has successfully given an operational semantics for such a language in a multi-step style with "tags" indicating current points of computation. However, this operational semantics is sufficiently different from those given in this thesis that it would require a very different structure of soundness and completeness theorems.

2. Practical Program Proving

Program proving, the practice of proving useful properties of programs, has been studied for many years. I have made some reference to practical program proving in the course of this thesis, particularly in the section on induction; although optimisations would be needed for converting the proof systems given here into a practical tool for proving properties of logic programs, those proof systems do act as a basis for such a tool.

Most past program-proving research has gone on in the paradigms of imperative or functional programming. I feel that this may have been, in part, a result of the split between theory and practice in logic programming. Practical program proving is intended to apply to practical languages; the practical languages in logic programming are the sequential ones; and, until now, there has been no satisfactory logical account of sequential logic programming. The closest we have come to program proving of sequential logic programs has been the operational work of Francez et al. [34] and Baudinet's translation of logic programs into functional programs to be proven with known functional tools [12]. The contributions in this thesis go some way towards filling this gap between theory and practice.

Past experience in other paradigms can help research into logic program proving. But besides the usual scientific motivations of wanting to apply given knowledge to a new area of study, there are important considerations to do with methodology of programming in this area of research.

Logic programs are often compared to "executable specifications"; the logical outlook we need to write logic programs carries over to the process of proving program properties. It may be, therefore, that it would be easier to prove properties of logic programs than of imperative or functional programs, if we had the appropriate tools. Tools to assist or automatically generate proofs of logic programs would serve to test this hypothesis and investigate its consequences.

Tools for proving properties of logic programs would not necessarily be very useful by themselves. They would be more useful in the context of a comprehensive logic program development environment. Mello and Natali [53] discuss such an environment, Contextual Prolog, which lacks a theorem prover but provides the necessary tools for refinement of prototype programs. It would be interesting to see how this or other approaches to development could benefit from a proof assistant system.

Bibliography

[1] James H. Andrews. An environment theory with precomplete negation over pairs. Technical Report 86-23, University of British Columbia, Department of Computer Science, Vancouver, B. C., 1986.

[2] James H. Andrews. *Trilogy Users' Manual.* Complete Logic Systems, Inc., Vancouver, B.C., Canada, 1987.

[3] James H. Andrews. Predicates as parameters in logic programming: A set-theoretic basis. In *Proceedings of Workshop on Extensions to Logic Programming*, volume 475 of *Lecture Notes in Artificial Intelligence*, pages 31–47, Tübingen, Germany, December 1989. Springer.

[4] James H. Andrews. Proof-theoretic characterisations of logic programming. Technical Report LFCS-89-77, Laboratory for the Foundations of Computer Science, University of Edinburgh, Edinburgh, Scotland, May 1989.

[5] James H. Andrews. Proof-theoretic characterisations of logic programming. In *Proceedings of the 14th International Symposium on the Mathematical Foundations of Computer Science*, volume 379 of *Lecture Notes in Computer Science*, pages 145–154, Porąbka-Kozubnik, Poland, August-September 1989. Springer.

[6] James H. Andrews. The logical structure of sequential Prolog. Technical Report LFCS-90-110, Laboratory for the Foundations of Computer Science, University of Edinburgh, Edinburgh, Scotland, April 1990.

[7] James H. Andrews. The logical structure of sequential Prolog. In *Proceedings of the 1990 North American Conference on Logic Programming*, pages 585–602, Austin, Texas, October-November 1990. MIT Press.

[8] Krzysztof R. Apt, Roland N. Bol, and Jan Willem Klop. On the safe termination of Prolog programs. In *Proceedings of the Sixth International Conference on Logic Programming*, pages 353–368, Lisbon, 1989.

[9] Bijan Arbab and Daniel M. Berry. Operational and denotational semantics of Prolog. *Journal of Logic Programming*, 4:309–329, 1987.

[10] Edward Babb. An incremental pure logic language with constraints and classical negation. In Tony Dodd, Richard Owens, and Steve Torrance, editors, *Logic Programming: Expanding the Horizons*, pages 14–62, Oxford, 1991. Intellect.

[11] Henk Barendregt. *The Lambda Calculus: Its Syntax and Semantics*, volume 103 of *Studies in Logic and Foundations of Mathematics*. North-Holland, Amsterdam, 1984.

[12] Marianne Baudinet. Proving termination properties of Prolog programs: A semantic approach. In *Proceedings of the Third Annual IEEE Symposium on Logic in Computer Science*, pages 336–347, Edinburgh, Scotland, July 1988.

[13] Egon Börger. A logical operational semantics of full Prolog. Technical Report IWBS Report 111, IBM Wissenschaftliches Zentrum, Institut für Wissensbasierte Systeme, Heidelberg, Germany, March 1990.

[14] A. Bossi and N. Cocco. Verifying correctness of logic programs. In *Theory and Practice of Software Engineering*, volume 352 of *Lecture Notes in Computer Science*, pages 96–110, Barcelona, Spain, 1989. Springer-Verlag.

[15] Julian Bradfield and Colin Stirling. Local model checking for infinite state spaces. Technical Report LFCS-90-115, Laboratory for the Foundations of Computer Science, University of Edinburgh, Edinburgh, 1990.

[16] R. M. Burstall. Proving properties of programs by structural induction. *Computer Journal*, 12(1):41–48, 1969.

[17] R. M. Burstall and J. Darlington. A transformation system for developing recursive programs. *Journal of the ACM*, 24(1):44–67, 1977.

[18] Luca Cardelli and Peter Wegner. On understanding types, data abstraction, and polymorphism. *ACM Computing Surveys*, 17(4):471–522, December 1985.

[19] Weidong Chen, Michael Kifer, and David S. Warren. HiLog: A first-order semantics of higher-order logic programming constructs. In *Proceedings of the North American Conference on Logic Programming*, Cleveland, Ohio, October 1989.

[20] Alonzo Church. *Introduction to Mathematical Logic*. Princeton University Press, Princeton, New Jersey, 1956.

[21] K. L. Clark. Negation as failure. In *Logic and Data Bases*, pages 293–322, New York, 1978. Plenum Press.

[22] K. L. Clark. Predicate logic as a computational formalism. Technical Report 79/59 TOC, Department of Computing, Imperial College, London, December 1979.

[23] K. L. Clark and S. Gregory. PARLOG: A parallel logic programming language. Technical Report DOC 83/5, Department of Computing, Imperial College, London, 1983.

[24] K. L. Clark and F. McCabe. The control facilities of IC-Prolog. In D. Michie, editor, *Expert Systems in the Micro-Electronic Age*, pages 122–149. Edinburgh University Press, 1983.

[25] Alain Colmerauer, Henry Kanoui, and Michel van Caneghem. Prolog, theoretical principles and current trends. *Technology and Science of Information*, 2(4):255–292, 1983.

[26] A. de Bruin and E. P. de Vink. Continuation semantics for Prolog with cut. In *Theory and Practice of Software Engineering*, volume 351 of *Lecture Notes in Computer Science*, pages 178–192, Barcelona, Spain, 1989. Springer-Verlag.

[27] Saumya Debray and Prateek Mishra. Denotational and operational semantics of Prolog. *Journal of Logic Programming*, 5:61–91, 1988.

[28] Saumya K. Debray and David S. Warren. Automatic mode inference for Prolog programs. In *Proceedings of 1986 Symposium on Logic Programming*, pages 78–88, Salt Lake City, Utah, September 1983.

[29] P. Deransart and G. Ferrand. An operational formal definition of Prolog. Technical Report RR763, INRIA, 1987.

[30] Pierre Deransart. Proofs of declarative properties of logic programs. In *Theory and Practice of Software Engineering*, volume 351 of *Lecture Notes in Computer Science*, pages 207–226, Barcelona, Spain, 1989. Springer-Verlag.

[31] Yves Deville. *Logic Programming: Systematic Program Development.* Addison-Wesley, Wokingham, England, 1990.

[32] Frederic Brenton Fitch. *Symbolic Logic: An Introduction.* Ronald Press, New York, 1952.

[33] Melvin Fitting. A Kripke-Kleene semantics for logic programs. *Journal of Logic Programming*, 4:295–312, 1985.

[34] N. Francez, O. Grumberg, S. Katz, and A. Pnueli. Proving termination of Prolog programs. In Rohit Parikh, editor, *Logics of Programs*, volume 193 of *Lecture Notes in Computer Science*, pages 89–105, Berlin, July 1985. Springer-Verlag.

[35] D. M. Gabbay and U. Reyle. N-Prolog: An extension of Prolog with hypothetical implications, i. *Journal of Logic Programming*, 1:319–355, 1984.

[36] Gerhardt Gentzen. *The Collected Papers of Gerhard Gentzen.* North-Holland, Amsterdam, 1969. Ed. M. E. Szabo.

[37] Paul C. Gilmore. Natural deduction based set theories: A new resolution of the old paradoxes. *Journal of Symbolic Logic*, 51(2):393–411, June 1986.

[38] Jean-Yves Girard. Towards a geometry of interaction. In *Proceedings of the AMS Conference on Categories, Logic, and Computer Science*, Boulder, Colorado, June 1987. To appear.

[39] Kurt Gödel. *On Formally Undecidable Propositions of Principia Mathematica and Related Systems.* Oliver and Boyd, Edinburgh, 1962. Translation by B. Meltzer of "Über formal unentscheidbare Sätze der Principia Mathematica und verwandter Systeme I", *Monatshefte für Mathematik und Physik*, 38:173-198, Leipzig, 1931.

[40] Robert Goldblatt. *Axiomatising the Logic of Computer Programming*, volume 130 of *Lecture Notes in Computer Science*. Springer-Verlag, Berlin, 1982.

[41] Masami Hagiya and Takafumi Sakurai. Foundation of logic programming based on inductive definition. *New Generation Computing*, 2:59–77, 1984.

[42] Lars Hallnäs and Peter Schroeder-Heister. A proof-theoretic approach to logic programming. Technical Report R88005, Swedish Institute of Computer Science, 1988.

[43] Seif Haridi and Sverker Janson. Kernel Andorra Prolog and its computation model. In *Proceedings of the International Conference on Logic Programming*, pages 31–46, Jerusalem, 1990.

[44] Jacques Herbrand. Researches in the theory of demonstration. In J. van Heijenoort, editor, *From Frege to Gödel: A Source Book in Mathematical Logic, 1879-1931*, pages 525–581, Boston, 1930. Harvard University Press.

[45] Robert Hill. LUSH-resolution and its completeness. Technical Report DCI Memo 78, Department of Artificial Intelligence, University of Edinburgh, Edinburgh, 1974.

[46] Joxan Jaffar and Jean-Louis Lassez. Constraint logic programming. Technical report, Department of Computer Science, Monash University, June 1986.

[47] Joxan Jaffar, Jean-Louis Lassez, and John Lloyd. Completeness of the negation as failure rule. In *Proceedings of the International Joint Conference on Artificial Intelligence*, pages 500–506, Karlsruhe, 1983.

[48] Neil D. Jones and Alan Mycroft. Stepwise development of operational and denotational semantics for Prolog. In *Proceedings of the 1984 International Symposium on Logic Programming*, February 1984.

[49] Robert Kowalski. Predicate logic as programming language. In *Information Processing 74 - Proceedings of the IFIP Conference*. North-Holland, 1974.

[50] John W. Lloyd. *Foundations of Logic Programming*. Springer-Verlag, Berlin, 1984.

[51] Zohar Manna and Richard Waldinger. The logic of computer programming. *IEEE Transactions on Software Engineering*, SE-4:199–229, 1978.

[52] Peter McBrien. Implementing logic languages by graph rewriting. In Tony Dodd, Richaard Owens, and Steve Torrance, editors, *Logic Programming: Expanding the Horizons*, pages 164–188, Oxford, 1991. Intellect.

[53] Paola Mello and Antonio Natali. Logic programming in a software engineering perspective. In *Proceedings of the 1989 North American Conference on Logic Programming*, pages 441–458, Cleveland, Ohio, 1989.

[54] Dale Miller, Gopalan Nadathur, and Andre Scedrov. Hereditary harrop formulas and uniform proof systems. Technical Report MS-CIS-87-24, Department of Computer and Information Science, University of Pennsylvania, Philadelphia, March 1987.

[55] Dale A. Miller and Gopalan Nadathur. Higher-order logic programming. In *Proceedings of the Third International Logic Programming Conference*, Imperial College, London, July 1986.

[56] Lee Naish. *MU-Prolog 3.1db Reference Manual.* University of Melbourne, 1984.

[57] Tim Nicholson and Norman Foo. A denotational semantics for Prolog. *ACM Transactions on Programming Languages and Systems*, 11:650–665, October 1989.

[58] Gordon Plotkin. A structural approach to operational semantics. Technical Report DAIMI FN-19, Computer Science Department, Aarhus University, Aarhus, September 1981.

[59] Lutz Plümer. *Termination Proofs for Logic Programs*, volume 446 of *Lecture Notes in Artificial Intelligence.* Springer-Verlag, Berlin, 1990.

[60] Lutz Plümer. Termination proofs for logic programs based on predicate inequalities. In *Proceedings of the 1990 International Conference on Logic Programming*, pages 634–648, Jerusalem, July 1990.

[61] David Poole and Randy Goebel. On eliminating loops in Prolog. *SIGPLAN Notices*, 20(8):38–40, 1985.

[62] Dag Prawitz. An improved proof procedure. *Theoria*, 26:102–139, 1960.

[63] Dag Prawitz. *Natural Deduction: A Proof-Theoretical Study*, volume 3 of *Acta Universitatis Stockholmiensis, Stockholm Studies in Philosophy.* Almqvist and Wiksell, Uppsala, 1965.

[64] Changwoo Pyo and Uday S. Reddy. Inference of polymorphic types for logic programs. In *Proceedings of the 1989 North American Conference on Logic Programming*, pages 1115–1132, Cleveland, Ohio, 1989.

[65] Uday S. Reddy. Types in logic programming. Austin, Texas, October-November 1988. Notes for tutorial given at the North American Conference on Logic Programming.

[66] J. Alan Robinson. A machine-oriented logic based on the resolution principle. *Journal of the Association for Computing Machinery*, 12:23–41, 1965.

[67] Ehud Shapiro. The family of concurrent logic programming languages. *ACM Computing Surveys*, 21(3):412–510, September 1989.

[68] Ehud Shapiro and Akikazu Takeuchi. Object oriented programming in Concurrent Prolog. *New Generation Computing*, 1(1), 1983.

[69] Joseph Shoenfield. *Mathematical Logic.* Addison-Wesley, Reading, Mass., 1967.

[70] Joseph E. Stoy. *Denotational Semantics: The Scott-Strachey Approach to Programming Language Theory.* The MIT Press, Cambridge, Massachusetts, 1977.

[71] Göran Sundholm. Systems of deduction. In D. Gabbay and F. Guenther, editors, *Handbook of Philosophical Logic*, pages 133–188. D. Reidel, Dordrecht, 1983.

[72] Gaisi Takeuti. *Proof Theory*. North-Holland, Amsterdam, 1987.

[73] H. Tamaki and T. Sato. Unfold/fold transformations of logic programs. In *Proceedings of the Second International Logic Programming Conference*, pages 127–138, Uppsala, Sweden, 1984.

[74] Maarten H. van Emden and Robert A. Kowalski. The semantics of predicate logic as a programming language. *Journal of the Association for Computing Machinery*, 23(4):733–742, October 1976.

[75] Allen van Gelder. Efficient loop detection in Prolog using the tortoise-and-hare technique. *Journal of Logic Programming*, 4:23–31, 1987.

[76] Paul J. Voda. A view of programming languages as symbiosis of meaning and computations. *New Generation Computing*, 3:71–100, 1985.

Appendix A

Examples

1. Conventions

Computations in this appendix of examples will appear in the following format: with the starting backtrack stack on a line by itself, and then each step on a separate line or lines consisting of the number of the computation rule from the relevant SOS variant, the production arrow, and the resultant backtrack stack. For example, in the computation

$$
\begin{array}{ll}
 & (() : (Loop()\&false) \lor true) \\
(2) & \overset{\mathrm{SOS/so}}{\Rightarrow} (() : Loop()\&false); (() : true) \\
(1) & \overset{\mathrm{SOS/so}}{\Rightarrow} (() : Loop(), false); (() : true) \\
\ldots &
\end{array}
$$

the second backtrack stack is derived from the first by an application of rule 2 ($\lor$) from SOS/so; the third is derived from the second by an application of rule 1 (&) from SOS/so; and so on.

Due to formatting difficulties, the example derivations in this appendix will not be of the tree format in which the rules are given. They will be instead in the following style: each sequent will be given on a separate line, with the premisses in the derivation of each sequent being above it and indented. Dots will be placed on each line to help the reader see the indentation.

Thus the derivation which is written in tree style as

$$
\dfrac{\dfrac{\overline{\mathrm{A}} \quad \overline{\mathrm{B}}}{\mathrm{E}} \qquad \dfrac{\overline{\mathrm{C}} \quad \overline{\mathrm{D}}}{\mathrm{F}}}{\mathrm{G}}
$$

will appear in this appendix as something like the following:

. . A
. . B
. E
. . C
. . D
. F
G

2. List Membership Examples

These examples are based on the definition of the Mem predicate:

$$Mem(x,l) \leftrightarrow \exists h\, \exists t\, (l = [h|t] \& (x = h \vee Mem(x,t)))$$

The query we will be concerned with is $Mem(x, [a|[b|[\ ]]])$. I assume that $[\ ]$ is the nullary "empty list" constant and $[\ |\ ]$ is the binary list formation function symbol, and that a and b are constants. I will give the SP (sequential) computation of this query, then an alternate SOS computation which makes use of the parallel "or"; then I will give two derivations in LKE+PAR and two in LKE+SEQ for the query.

2.1. Computations

The SP computation for the query is in Figure A.1. The computation ends with the solution a for x.

One possible SOS-computation starts off the same, but then proceeds differently after the second-last step by expanding the predicate call in the second closure, ending with the solution b for x. This computation is given in Figure A.2.

Note the renaming that goes on in the second and third steps, the first renaming (of t to t_1) to avoid variable capture arising from the definition of substitution, and the second (from h to h_1) arising from the $\exists$ rule.

2.2. Derivations

The sequent corresponding to the statement that the query succeeds is the following one:

$$\rightarrow S(\exists x\, Mem(x, [a|[b|[\ ]]]))$$

In PAR, one possible derivation is given in Figure A.3. Only the essential steps are given; in particular, the major premisses of the numerous Cut rules are omitted. They can be easily guessed by inspection of the PAR axioms.

Another derivation, which corresponds to the second computation given above, is given in Figure A.4. The difference arises here only from a different choice of witness for x.

The more complex SEQ derivation is given in Figure A.5. Note that we must do a predicate and then a disjunctive unfolding to handle the predicate call in the query.

3. Infinite Loop

Here, we treat the slightly paradoxical example of the query which succeeds in all operational semantics except SP, but diverges in SP. The example is the query

$$(Loop() \& false) \vee true$$

where $false \equiv 0 = 1$, $true \equiv 0 = 0$, and $Loop$ is defined with the predicate definition

$$Loop() \leftrightarrow Loop()$$

The computation of this query in SOS/so is in Figure A.6.

There is no terminating SP computation of the query; the computation sequence just loops on the predicate call. See Figure A.7 for this computation.

$$
\begin{array}{ll}
 & ((): Mem(x,[a|[b|[\,]]])\\
(4) & \overset{\text{SP}}{\Rightarrow} ((): \exists h\, \exists t\, ([a|[b|[\,]]] = [h|t] \& (x = h \vee Mem(x,t))))\\
(3) & \overset{\text{SP}}{\Rightarrow} ((): \exists t\, ([a|[b|[\,]]] = [h|t] \& (x = h \vee Mem(x,t))))\\
(3) & \overset{\text{SP}}{\Rightarrow} ((): [a|[b|[\,]]] = [h|t] \& (x = h \vee Mem(x,t))))\\
(1) & \overset{\text{SP}}{\Rightarrow} ((): [a|[b|[\,]]] = [h|t], x = h \vee Mem(x,t)))\\
(5) & \overset{\text{SP}}{\Rightarrow} ([h := a, t := [b|[\,]]] : x = h \vee Mem(x,t)))\\
(2) & \overset{\text{SP}}{\Rightarrow} ([h := a, t := [b|[\,]]] : x = h); ([h := a, t := [b|[\,]]] : Mem(x,t))\\
(5) & \overset{\text{SP}}{\Rightarrow} ([h := a, t := [b|[\,]], x := a] : \epsilon); ([h := a, t := [b|[\,]]] : Mem(x,t))
\end{array}
$$

Figure A.1. The computation of the query $Mem(x,[a|[b|[\,]]])$ in SP.

$$
\begin{array}{ll}
\ldots & \\
(2) & \overset{\text{SQS}}{\Rightarrow} ([h := a, t := [b|[\,]]] : x = h); ([h := a, t := [b|[\,]]] : Mem(x,t))\\
(4) & \overset{\text{SQS}}{\Rightarrow} ([h := a, t := [b|[\,]]] : x = h);\\
 & \quad ([h := a, t := [b|[\,]]] : \exists h\, \exists t_1\, (t = [h|t_1] \& (x = h \vee Mem(x,t_1))))\\
(3) & \overset{\text{SQS}}{\Rightarrow} ([h := a, t := [b|[\,]]] : x = h);\\
 & \quad ([h := a, t := [b|[\,]]] : \exists t_1\, (t = [h_1|t_1] \& (x = h_1 \vee Mem(x,t_1))))\\
(3) & \overset{\text{SQS}}{\Rightarrow} ([h := a, t := [b|[\,]]] : x = h);\\
 & \quad ([h := a, t := [b|[\,]]] : t = [h_1|t_1] \& (x = h_1 \vee Mem(x,t_1)))\\
(1) & \overset{\text{SQS}}{\Rightarrow} ([h := a, t := [b|[\,]]] : x = h);\\
 & \quad ([h := a, t := [b|[\,]]] : t = [h_1|t_1], x = h_1 \vee Mem(x,t_1))\\
(5) & \overset{\text{SQS}}{\Rightarrow} ([h := a, t := [b|[\,]]] : x = h);\\
 & \quad ([h := a, t := [b|[\,]], h_1 := b, t_1 = [\,]] : x = h_1 \vee Mem(x,t_1))\\
(2) & \overset{\text{SQS}}{\Rightarrow} ([h := a, t := [b|[\,]]] : x = h);\\
 & \quad ([h := a, t := [b|[\,]], h_1 := b, t_1 = [\,]] : x = h_1);\\
 & \quad ([h := a, t := [b|[\,]], h_1 := b, t_1 = [\,]] : Mem(x,t_1))\\
(5) & \overset{\text{SQS}}{\Rightarrow} ([h := a, t := [b|[\,]]] : x = h);\\
 & \quad ([h := a, t := [b|[\,]], h_1 := b, t_1 = [\,], x = b] : \epsilon);\\
 & \quad ([h := a, t := [b|[\,]], h_1 := b, t_1 = [\,]] : Mem(x,t_1))
\end{array}
$$

Figure A.2. One possible computation of the query $Mem(x,[a|[b|[\,]]])$ in SOS; the first step shown is the second last of the SP computation.

$$
\begin{array}{l}
\cdot\ \cdot\ \cdot\ \cdot\ \cdot\ \cdot\ \rightarrow S([a|[b|[\,]]] = [a|[b|[\,]]])\\
\cdot\ \cdot\ \cdot\ \cdot\ \cdot\ \cdot\ \cdot\ \rightarrow S(a = a)\\
\cdot\ \cdot\ \cdot\ \cdot\ \cdot\ \cdot\ \rightarrow S(a = a \vee Mem(a|[b|[\,]]))\\
\cdot\ \cdot\ \cdot\ \cdot\ \cdot\ \rightarrow S([a|[b|[\,]]] = [a|[b|[\,]]] \& (a = a \vee Mem(a,[b|[\,]])))\\
\cdot\ \cdot\ \cdot\ \cdot\ \rightarrow S(\exists t\, ([a|[b|[\,]]] = [a|t] \& (a = a \vee Mem(a,t))))\\
\cdot\ \cdot\ \cdot\ \rightarrow S(\exists h\, \exists t\, ([a|[b|[\,]]] = [h|t] \& (a = h \vee Mem(a,t))))\\
\cdot\ \rightarrow S(Mem(a,[a|[b|[\,]]]))\\
\rightarrow S(\exists x\, Mem(x,[a|[b|[\,]]]))
\end{array}
$$

Figure A.3. A derivation of the sequent $[\rightarrow S(\exists x\, Mem(x,[a|[b|[\,]]]))]$ in LKE+PAR. Only essential steps are given.

$$
\begin{array}{l}
\quad\quad\quad\quad\quad\quad\quad\quad\quad\quad\quad\quad . \ . \ . \ . \ . \ . \ . \rightarrow S([a|[b|[\,]]] = [a|[b|[\,]]]) \\
. \ . \ . \ . \ . \ . \ . \ . \ . \ . \ . \ . \rightarrow S([b|[\,]] = [b|[\,]]) \\
. \ . \ . \ . \ . \ . \ . \ . \ . \ . \ . \ . \ . \rightarrow S(b = b) \\
. \ . \ . \ . \ . \ . \ . \ . \ . \ . \ . \ . \rightarrow S(b = b \vee Mem(b,[\,])) \\
. \ . \ . \ . \ . \ . \ . \ . \ . \ . \ . \rightarrow S([b|[\,]] = [b|[\,]] \& (b = b \vee Mem(b,[\,]))) \\
. \ . \ . \ . \ . \ . \ . \ . \ . \ . \rightarrow S(\exists t\, ([b|[\,]] = [b|t] \& (b = b \vee Mem(b,t)))) \\
. \ . \ . \ . \ . \ . \ . \ . \ . \rightarrow S(\exists h\, \exists t\, ([b|[\,]] = [h|t] \& (b = h \vee Mem(b,t)))) \\
. \ . \ . \ . \ . \ . \ . \ . \rightarrow S(Mem(b,[b|[\,]])) \\
. \ . \ . \ . \ . \ . \ . \rightarrow S(b = a \vee Mem(a,[b|[\,]])) \\
. \ . \ . \ . \ . \ . \rightarrow S([a|[b|[\,]]] = [a|[b|[\,]]] \& (b = a \vee Mem(b,[b|[\,]]))) \\
. \ . \ . \ . \rightarrow S(\exists t\, ([a|[b|[\,]]] = [a|t] \& (b = a \vee Mem(b,t)))) \\
. \ . \ . \rightarrow S(\exists h\, \exists t\, ([a|[b|[\,]]] = [h|t] \& (b = h \vee Mem(b,t)))) \\
. \ . \rightarrow S(Mem(b,[a|[b|[\,]]])) \\
\rightarrow S(\exists x\, Mem(x,[a|[b|[\,]]]))
\end{array}
$$

Figure A.4. Another derivation of the sequent $[\rightarrow S(\exists x\, Mem(x,[a|[b|[\,]]]))]$ in LKE+PAR. Only essential steps are given.

$$
\begin{array}{l}
. \ . \ . \ . \ . \ . \ . \ . \ . \ . \ . \rightarrow S([a|[b|[\,]]] = [a|[b|[\,]]]) \\
. \ . \ . \ . \ . \ . \ . \ . \ . \ . \ . \rightarrow S(a = a) \\
. \ . \ . \ . \ . \ . \ . \ . \ . \ . \rightarrow S(([a|[b|[\,]]] = [a|[b|[\,]]] \& a = a)) \\
. \ . \ . \ . \ . \ . \ . \ . \rightarrow S(\exists t\, ([a|[b|[\,]]] = [a|t] \& a = a)) \\
. \ . \ . \ . \ . \ . \ . \rightarrow S(\exists h\, \exists t\, ([a|[b|[\,]]] = [h|t] \& a = h)) \\
. \ . \ . \ . \ . \rightarrow S(\exists x\, \exists h\, \exists t\, (\mathbf{B})) \\
. \ . \ . \ . \rightarrow S(\exists x\, \exists h\, \exists t\, (\mathbf{B})) \vee (F(\exists x\, \exists h\, \exists t\, (\mathbf{B})) \& S(\exists x\, \exists h\, \exists t\, (\mathbf{C}))) \\
. \ . \ . \rightarrow S(\exists x\, \exists h\, \exists t\, (\mathbf{B}) \vee \exists x\, \exists h\, \exists t\, (\mathbf{C})) \\
. \ . \rightarrow S(\exists x\, \exists h\, \exists t\, ([a|[b|[\,]]] = [h|t] \& (x = h \vee Mem(x,t)))) \\
\rightarrow S(\exists x\, Mem(x,[a|[b|[\,]]]))
\end{array}
$$

where $\mathbf{B} \equiv ([a|[b|[\,]]] = [h|t] \& x = h)$ and $\mathbf{C} \equiv ([a|[b|[\,]]] = [h|t] \& Mem(x,t))$

Figure A.5. A derivation of the sequent $[\rightarrow S(\exists x\, Mem(x,[a|[b|[\,]]]))]$ in LKE+SEQ. Only essential steps are given.

$$
\begin{array}{ll}
 & ((): (Loop() \& false) \vee true) \\
(2) & \overset{SOS/so}{\Rightarrow} ((): Loop() \& false); ((): true) \\
(1) & \overset{SOS/so}{\Rightarrow} ((): Loop(), false); ((): true) \\
(6) & \overset{SOS/so}{\Rightarrow} ((): true) \\
(5) & \overset{SOS/so}{\Rightarrow} (():)
\end{array}
$$

Figure A.6. Computation of query $(Loop() \& false) \vee true$ in SOS/so.

3.1. Derivations

To see that $(Loop()\&false) \vee true$ succeeds in SOS (or SOS/sa, since its set of successful queries is the same), we need only give the derivation for the sequent

$$[\to S((Loop()\&false) \vee true)]$$

in LKE+PAR. This derivation is in Figure A.8.

It is only slightly more complex to prove that it succeeds in SOS/so, by giving the LKE+PASO derivation for the query. (Recall that PASO takes the success rules from SEQ and the failure rules from PAR.) See Figure A.9 for this derivation.

However, as we would expect, it is impossible to give a derivation of the sequent in SEQ. Any such derivation would involve a derivation of $[\to F(Loop()\&false)]$, which can be proven in turn only by proving $[\to F(Loop())]$. This is clearly impossible.

4. Subterm Induction

The example to be proven here is the sequent

$$\to S(Add(x, 0, x))$$

– that is, "for all terms **t**, the query $Add(\mathbf{t}, 0, \mathbf{t})$ succeeds", where *Add* is defined as follows:

$$\begin{aligned} Add(x, y, z) \leftrightarrow\ & (x = 0 \& y = z) \\ \vee\ & \exists px, pz(x = s(px)\ \&\ Add(px, y, pz)\ \&\ z = s(pz)) \end{aligned}$$

This is true only if we make some assumptions about the language. We will assume that the language contains only the unary function symbol s, and the constant (nullary function symbol) 0. See Figure A.10 for the derivation of this sequent in LKE+PAR+SUBTERM.

5. Well-Founded Induction

The example to be proven here is the analogue of the sequent in the last section:

$$\to S(N(y)) \supset S(Add(y, 0, y))$$

– that is, "for all terms **t** such that $N(\mathbf{t})$ succeeds, the query $Add(\mathbf{t}, 0, \mathbf{t})$ succeeds". The definitions of N, the predicate testing for whether its argument is a Peano natural number, the order predicate, R, and its auxiliary predicate Lt, are as follows:

$$N(x) \leftrightarrow x = 0 \vee \exists px(x = s(px) \& N(px))$$

$$R(x, y) \leftrightarrow N(x) \& N(y) \& Lt(x, y)$$

$$Lt(x, y) \leftrightarrow \exists py(y = s(py) \& (x = py \vee Lt(x, py)))$$

We now need no assumptions on the language (except, obviously, that it contains 0 and s). See Figures A.11 and A.12 for the derivation of this sequent in LKE+PAR+WF.

$$
\begin{array}{ll}
 & (() : (Loop()\&false) \vee true) \\
(2) & \stackrel{SP}{\Rightarrow} (() : Loop()\&false); (() : true) \\
(1) & \stackrel{SP}{\Rightarrow} (() : Loop(), false); (() : true) \\
(4) & \stackrel{SP}{\Rightarrow} (() : Loop(), false); (() : true) \\
(4) & \stackrel{SP}{\Rightarrow} (() : Loop(), false); (() : true) \\
(4) & \stackrel{SP}{\Rightarrow} \dots
\end{array}
$$

Figure A.7. First part of infinite computation sequence of query $(Loop()\&false) \vee true$ in SP.

$$
\begin{array}{l}
.\ .\ \rightarrow 0 = 0 \\
.\ \rightarrow S(true) \\
\rightarrow S((Loop()\&false) \vee true)
\end{array}
$$

Figure A.8. Derivation of $[\rightarrow S((Loop()\&false) \vee true)]$ in LKE+PAR. Only essential steps are given.

$$
\begin{array}{l}
.\ .\ .\ .\ .\ .\ .\ .\ 0 = 1 \rightarrow \\
.\ .\ .\ .\ .\ .\ .\ \rightarrow \neg 0 = 1 \\
.\ .\ .\ .\ .\ .\ \rightarrow F(false) \\
.\ .\ .\ .\ .\ \rightarrow F(Loop()) \vee F(false) \\
.\ .\ .\ .\ \rightarrow F(Loop()\&false) \\
.\ .\ .\ .\ .\ \rightarrow 0 = 0 \\
.\ .\ .\ .\ \rightarrow S(true) \\
.\ .\ \rightarrow F(Loop()\&false)\&S(true) \\
.\ \rightarrow S(Loop()\&false) \vee (F(Loop()\&false)\&S(true)) \\
\rightarrow S((Loop()\&false) \vee true)
\end{array}
$$

Figure A.9. Derivation of $[\rightarrow S((Loop()\&false) \vee true)]$ in LKE+PASO. Only essential steps are given.

$$
\begin{array}{l}
.\ .\ .\ .\ .\ \rightarrow S(0 = 0) \\
.\ .\ .\ .\ .\ \rightarrow S(0 = 0) \\
.\ .\ .\ .\ \rightarrow S(0 = 0\&0 = 0) \\
.\ .\ .\ \rightarrow S((0 = 0\&0 = 0) \vee \dots) \\
.\ \rightarrow S(Add(0, 0, 0)) \\
.\ .\ .\ .\ .\ .\ \rightarrow S(s(x) = s(x)) \\
.\ .\ .\ .\ .\ .\ .\ S(Add(x, 0, x)) \rightarrow S(Add(x, 0, x)) \\
.\ .\ .\ .\ .\ .\ .\ \rightarrow S(s(x) = s(x)) \\
.\ .\ .\ .\ .\ .\ S(Add(x, 0, x)) \rightarrow S(Add(x, 0, x)\&s(x) = s(x)) \\
.\ .\ .\ .\ .\ S(Add(x, 0, x)) \rightarrow S(s(x) = s(x)\&Add(x, 0, x)\&s(x) = s(x)) \\
.\ .\ .\ .\ S(Add(x, 0, x)) \rightarrow S(\exists px, pz(\dots)) \\
.\ .\ .\ S(Add(x, 0, x)) \rightarrow S((s(x) = 0\&0 = s(x)) \vee \exists px, pz(\dots)) \\
.\ S(Add(x, 0, x)) \rightarrow S(Add(s(x), 0, s(x))) \\
\rightarrow S(Add(x, 0, x))
\end{array}
$$

Figure A.10. Derivation of $[\rightarrow S(Add(x, 0, x))]$ in LKE+PAR+SUBTERM. Only essential rule applications are shown.

. . . . (as in subterm induction example)
. . . . $\rightarrow S(Add(0,0,0))$
. . . . $\mathbf{B}(0), \rightarrow S(Add(0,0,0))$
. . . . . . $\mathbf{B}(y), S(y=0) \rightarrow S(Add(y,0,y))$
. . . . (see next figure)
. . . . $\mathbf{B}(y), S(y=s(py)\&N(py)) \rightarrow S(Add(y,0,y))$
. . . . . . $\mathbf{B}(y), S(\exists px(y=s(px)\&N(px))) \rightarrow S(Add(y,0,y))$
. . . . . $\mathbf{B}(y), S(y=0) \vee S(\exists px(\ldots)) \rightarrow S(Add(y,0,y))$
. . . . $\mathbf{B}(y), S(y=0 \vee \exists px(y=s(px)\&N(px))) \rightarrow S(Add(y,0,y))$
. . . $\mathbf{B}(y), S(N(y)) \rightarrow S(Add(y,0,y))$
. . $\mathbf{B}(y) \rightarrow \mathbf{C}(y)$
$\rightarrow \mathbf{C}(y)$

where $\mathbf{C}(\mathbf{z}) \equiv S(N(\mathbf{z})) \supset S(Add(\mathbf{z},0,\mathbf{z}))$ and $\mathbf{B}(\mathbf{z}) \equiv \forall x(S(R(x,\mathbf{z})) \supset \mathbf{C}(\mathbf{z}))$

Figure A.11. Derivation of $\rightarrow S(N(y)) \supset S(Add(y,0,y))$ in LKE+PAR+WF. The derivation of $\mathbf{B}(y), S(y=s(py)\&N(py)) \rightarrow S(Add(y,0,y))$ is in the next figure.

. . . . $S(N(py)) \rightarrow S(N(py))$
. . . . (straightforward)
. . . . $S(N(py)) \rightarrow S(N(s(py)))$
. . . . (straightforward)
. . . . $\rightarrow S(Lt(py,s(py)))$
. . . . $S(N(py)) \rightarrow S(Lt(py,s(py)))$
. . . . $S(N(py)) \rightarrow S(N(s(py))\&Lt(py,s(py)))$
. . . . $S(N(py)) \rightarrow S(N(py)\&N(s(py))\&Lt(py,s(py)))$
. . . . $S(N(py)) \rightarrow S(R(py,s(py))$
. . . . . . $S(N(py)) \rightarrow S(R(py,s(py)), S(Add(s(py),0,s(py)))$
. . . . (as in subterm induction example)
. . . . $S(Add(py,0,py)) \rightarrow S(Add(s(py),0,s(py)))$
. . . . $S(Add(py,0,py)), S(N(py)) \rightarrow S(Add(s(py),0,s(py)))$
. . . . $S(N(py)) \rightarrow S(N(py)), S(Add(s(py),0,s(py)))$
. . . . . . $\mathbf{C}(py), S(N(py)) \rightarrow S(Add(s(py),0,s(py)))$
. . . . . $S(R(py,s(py)) \supset \mathbf{C}(py), S(N(py)) \rightarrow S(Add(s(py),0,s(py)))$
. . . . $S(R(py,y)) \supset \mathbf{C}(py), S(y=s(py)), S(N(py)) \rightarrow S(Add(y,0,y))$
. . . $S(R(py,y)) \supset \mathbf{C}(py), S(y=s(py)\&N(py)) \rightarrow S(Add(y,0,y))$
$\mathbf{B}(y), S(y=s(py)\&N(py)) \rightarrow S(Add(y,0,y))$

where $\mathbf{C}(\mathbf{z}) \equiv S(N(\mathbf{z})) \supset S(Add(\mathbf{z},0,\mathbf{z}))$ and $\mathbf{B}(\mathbf{z}) \equiv \forall x(S(R(x,\mathbf{z})) \supset \mathbf{C}(\mathbf{z}))$

Figure A.12. Derivation of $\mathbf{B}(y), S(y = s(py)\&N(py)) \rightarrow S(Add(y,0,y))$ in LKE+PAR+WF.

Index of Definitions